# Answer Key
## An Introduction to Language

# 10e

**VICTORIA FROMKIN**
*Late, University of California, Los Angeles*

**ROBERT RODMAN**
*North Carolina State University, Raleigh*

**NINA HYAMS**
*University of California, Los Angeles*

**Prepared by Brook Danielle Lillehaugen**
*Haverford College*

WADSWORTH
CENGAGE Learning·

Australia • Brazil • Japan • Korea • Mexico • Singapore • Spain • United Kingdom • United States

# WADSWORTH
## CENGAGE Learning·

**Answer Key: An Introduction to Language, Tenth Edition**
Victoria Fromkin, Robert Rodman, Nina Hyams

Publisher: Michael Rosenberg

Development Editor: Joan M. Flaherty

Assistant Editor: Erin Bosco

Editorial Assistant: Rebecca Donahue

Media Editor: Janine Tangney

Market Development Manager:
Jason LaChapelle

Content Project Manager:
Dan Saabye

Art Director: Marissa Falco

Manufacturing Planner:
Betsy Donaghey

Rights Acquisition Specialist:
Jessica Elias

Production Service: PreMediaGlobal

Text Designer: Design and Production
Services

Cover Designer: Sarah Bishins Design

Cover Image: © 2009 Calder
Foundation, New York/Artists
Rights Society (ARS), New York.
Calder, Alexander (1898-1976)
© ARS, NY. Crinkly, 1970. Sheet
metal, wire, and paint. 71.1 x
166.4 x 30.5 cm. Location: Calder
Foundation, New York, NY, U.S.A.

Photo Credit: Calder Foundation,
New York/Art Resource, NY

Compositor: PreMediaGlobal

For product information and technology assistance, contact us at
**Cengage Learning Customer & Sales Support,**
**1-800-354-9706**

For permission to use material from this text or product, submit all requests online at **www.cengage.com/permissions.**
Further permissions questions can be emailed to
**permissionrequest@cengage.com.**

ISBN-13: 978-1-285-07978-3
ISBN-10: 1-285-07978-7

**Wadsworth**
20 Channel Center Street
Boston, MA 02210
USA

Cengage Learning is a leading provider of customized learning solutions with office locations around the globe, including Singapore, the United Kingdom, Australia, Mexico, Brazil and Japan. Locate your local office at **international.cengage.com/region**

Cengage Learning products are represented in Canada by Nelson Education, Ltd.

For your course and learning solutions, visit **www.cengage.com**. Purchase any of our products at your local college store or at our preferred online store **www.cengagebrain.com**.
**Instructors:** Please visit **login.cengage.com** and log in to access instructor-specific resources.

Printed in the United States of America
1 2 3 4 5 6 7 16 15 14 13

# Contents

# Chapter 1

1. *Sound sequences.* Any word that conforms to the sound pattern of English is a correct answer. For example:

   *Bliting: bl* as in *blood, iting* as in *lighting*
   *Krame: kr* as in *cream, ame* as in *aim*
   *Swirler: sw* as in *swim, irl* as in *girl, er* as in *rider*
   *Kristclean: kr* as in *cream, i* as in *pit, st* as in *street, clean* as in *clean*
   *Atla:* as in *atlas*
   *Oxfo: ox* as in *ox, fo* as in *foe*

   Existing English words as names of new products are also acceptable: for example, *Kleen* or *Clean* as the name of a laundry soap.

2. *Grammaticality judgments.* The following sentences are ungrammatical, but note that some judgments may vary across dialects:

   a. *\*Robin forced the sheriff go.*
      The word *to* is missing in front of the verb *go*. The verb *force* requires a *to* infinitive in the embedded clause.

   f. *\*He drove my house by.*
      Particles are preposition-like words that occur with verbs such as *look*, as in *look up the number* or *look over the data*. Particles can occur after their direct object: *look the number up; look the data over*. True prepositions do not behave this way. *He ran up the stairs* is grammatical, but *\*He ran the stairs up* is not. The *by* in *He drove by my house* functions as a preposition and may not occur after the direct object.

   g. *\*Did in a corner little Jack Horner sit?*
      You cannot turn a statement that begins with a prepositional phrase into a question. While you can form a question from *Little Jack Horner sat in a corner* with *Did little Jack Horner sit in a corner*, you cannot question the sentence *In a corner little Jack Horner sat.*

   h. *\*Elizabeth is resembled by Charles.*
      The verb *resemble* does not occur in passive sentences.

   k. *\*It is eager to love a kitten.*
      If the pronoun *it* refers to an animate (nonhuman) thing (e.g., a dog), the sentence is grammatical. If the word *it* is a "dummy subject," as

1

in *It's easy to love a kitten*, the sentence is ungrammatical because the adjective *eager* must have a referential subject.

l. *\*That birds can fly flabbergasts.*
*Flabbergast* is a transitive verb: it requires a direct object. Compare *That birds can fly flabbergasts John.*

n. *\*Has the nurse slept the baby yet?*
The verb *sleep* is intransitive: it cannot take a direct object (in this case, *the baby*).

o. *\*I was surprised for you to get married.*
The clause following the adjective *surprised* cannot be in the infinitive form, e.g., *to get*.

p. *\*I wonder who and Mary went swimming.*
This "question" is derived from the more basic sentence *Someone and Mary went swimming.* The coordinate structure constraint (see Chapter 3 for mention, but not a complete description) requires coordinate structures to be treated as a whole, not in part. So it is ungrammatical in most, but not all dialects of English, to ask *\*Who and Mary went swimming?* because there is an attempt to question one part, but not the other part, of the coordinate structure. This also explains the ungrammatical nature of *\*I wonder who and Mary went swimming* with similar caveats about dialectal and idiolectal variation.

q. *\*Myself bit John.*
Reflexive pronouns like *myself, yourself, herself, themselves,* etc., do not occur as subjects of sentences but only as objects, e.g., *John hurt himself.*

s. *\*What did Alice eat the toadstool and?*
A *wh-* phrase cannot be moved from inside a coordinate structure (e.g., *the toadstool and the fungi*) to form a *wh-* question.

3. *Onomatopoeic words.* Sample answers:

   *swish*—what you do when you ski

   *thunk*—the sound of a baseball hitting a mitt

   *scrunge*—the sound of a sponge wiping a table

   *glup*—the sound made when you swallow

   *squeeng*—the sound made when you pluck a taut elastic band

4. *Nonarbitrary and arbitrary signs.* Sample answers:

a. Nonarbitrary signs:
   - a picture of a knife and fork indicating a restaurant
   - the wheelchair sign that indicates disabled persons such as is used to reserve parking

- "No Smoking" sign with a slash through a burning cigarette
- "Do not Iron" sign on clothes depicting an iron with an X through it

b. Arbitrary signs:
- some gestures (e.g., a thumbs-up or a thumbs-down)
- stripes on military uniforms to represent different ranks
- a black armband for someone in mourning
- the U.S. zip code system
- some mathematical symbols (e.g., +, −, =)

5. *Learning.* The first statement (*I learned a new word today*) is quite probable. We constantly add to our vocabulary. In reading this book, for example, you may learn many new words. The second statement (*I learned a new sentence today*) is not very likely, since most sentences are not learned or memorized but rather constructed freely. Some sentences, such as slogans or sentences from a foreign language, may be learned as whole entities.

6. *Alex, the African grey parrot.* Answers will vary. Students may point out that Alex's ability to mimic human speech and the size of his vocabulary are quite impressive. They may further point out, however, that the ability to make human-like sounds and to memorize even a large number of words is not, in itself, language. The real question is not whether Alex can use human-like sounds to communicate, which he clearly can, but whether he has human language-like capabilities. Human language is an infinitely creative system made up of discrete, meaningful parts that may be combined in various ways. While Alex's talents are impressive, he can communicate only a small set of messages, while human language is infinitely creative in both the number and kinds of messages transmitted. There is no data demonstrating that Alex has any understanding or use of syntax. Without syntax, the communication system cannot be anything more than a communication system.

7. *Communication system of a wolf.* While a wolf's communication system is quite large and complex, it is finite and restricted to a limited set of messages within a single domain (the wolf's current emotions). Human language, on the other hand, is capable of expressing an infinite number of messages on any topic. Moreover, a wolf is unable to produce new messages using a different combination of independently meaningful gestures the way humans can.

8. *A dog's understanding of speech.* No. Even if the dog learned to respond to given cues to heel, sit up, beg, roll over, play dead, stay, jump, and bark in the correct way, it would not be learning language since its response would be driven solely by those cues. Such responses are stimulus-controlled

3

behavior. There is no creative aspect to the system: the dog could not associate a novel combination of cues with a complex action.

9. *"Correct" rules of grammar.* Here are some rules, often taught in English classes, which seem unnatural to many speakers:

   a. Never end a sentence with a preposition. Yet *What are you putting those marbles into?* is more common and natural for the majority of English speakers (including teachers of English) than *Into what are you putting those marbles?* English grammar permits the splitting of prepositional phrases.

   b. Don't split infinitives (i.e., don't insert anything between the infinitive marker *to* and the verb). However, a sentence such as *He was the first one to successfully climb Mount Everest* is grammatical.

   c. Use *whom* rather than *who* when the pronoun is the object of a verb or preposition, e.g., *Whom (rather than who) did you meet yesterday?* While this may have been part of the mental grammar of English speakers in the past, for most dialects the syntax has changed and *Who did you meet yesterday?* is the grammatical or "acceptable" structure.

   The essay may point out that a descriptive grammar describes speakers' basic linguistic knowledge while a prescriptive grammar postulates a set of rules that are considered "correct." Prescriptive grammarians often misunderstand the nature of language change and ignore the fact that all dialects are rule-governed and capable of expressing thought of any complexity.

10. *Comments on Chomsky's remark.* Chomsky believes that if apes were endowed with the ability to acquire language they would do so. The answer to this question should reflect an understanding of the studies presented in the chapter, which purport to show that the acquisition of language follows a pattern of development analogous to other kinds of biological development and is a result of a biological endowment specific to humans. The basis of the remark is in the fact that humans acquire language without instruction, while apes do not. (In fact, apes do not do so even with instruction.) The remark is also based on the assumption that the communication system used by apes is qualitatively different from human language; by "language ability" Chomsky means "human language ability." The analogy to flightless birds implies that learning to speak a language is like learning to fly—it is a property of the species. A species of birds that does not fly simply does not have the biological endowment to do so. An excellent expansion of this answer may be found in some of the works listed the references for Chapter 1, including Anderson 2008 and Bickerton 1990.

11. *Song titles.* Answers will vary. Some examples are:
    "Somethin' 'Bout a Truck" — Kip Moore
    "Why Ya Wanna" — Jana Kramer
    "Lemme See" — Usher

"(I Can't Get No) Satisfaction" — The Rolling Stones
"Gonna Make You Sweat" — C & C Music Factory
"We Gotta Get Out of This Place" — The Animals
"Ain't Too Proud to Beg" — The Temptations
"The Times They Are a-Changin'" — Bob Dylan

12. *Understanding the reality of a person's grammar.* Answers will vary. The essay might be along the lines of the following: Linguists who want to understand the reality of a person's grammar can learn by observing the utterances people make, and by deducing, perhaps by asking speakers, what kinds of utterances would not be made. The internal grammar must work so that it can produce all the possible sentences but none of the impossible ones. Linguists can hypothesize possible internal grammars, then see how well they perform at generating only the possible sentences. If the proposed grammar generates impossible sentences, or fails to generate possible ones, then it can be revised. In this way, linguists can develop increasingly sophisticated models of the internal grammars which speakers use. Linguists must take competence and performance into account so they distinguish between the possible *The very, very, very, very, very, very, very, very, very old man arrived late,* which is possible but nonoccurring, and *\*They swimmed in the pool,* which may occur as a slip of the tongue but is nonetheless not possible as a well-formed sentence.

13. *My Fair Lady.* One example is "The rain in Spain stays mainly in the plain," which is an attempt to get Eliza to pronounce the "long a" sound (indicated with the *ai* in *rain*) the way the upper classes pronounce it.

14. *Bilingualism.* Parts (a) and (b) are open-ended. For part (a), a student might observe that if the strong version of the Sapir-Whorf Hypothesis is true, then a bilingual person might be schizophrenic by having a dual world view forced on her by the two languages she knows. For part (b) a student might observe that an idiom such as the French *mariage de convenance* suggests that French speakers take marriage lightly. Students should consider both the strong and the weak versions of the Sapir-Whorf Hypothesis in answering.

   Part (c) should be "no"; i.e., you can always translate, even if it means a lot of circumlocution. But there may be connotations, or shades of meaning that are not easy to translate, so translating *le mot juste* from French into 'the right word' doesn't capture the connotation of it being the *perfectly* right word for the occasion.

15. *Pirahã.* Answers will vary. Readings will show that the Pirahã people do have difficulties doing quantitative comparisons with numbers larger than 6 or 8. However, in their culture there is little need for dealing with quantities in a precisely discrete manner, so it is questionable whether the language is influencing the culture, or vice versa. The same is true for color

5

terms, and the student reader may also learn that there are few if any kinship relation terms. However, in this case as well there may be a cultural explanation in that the people are so heavily intermarried that such terms probably wouldn't make much sense.

16. *British English words for woods and woodlands.*

    a. Answers will vary.

    b. Answers will vary. Students may discuss the meaning differences freely. The following definitions were found on dictionary.reference.com, except for the one marked with * which was found on www.merriam-webster.com/dictionary:

        bosky 'covered with bushes, shrubs, and small trees; woody'

        bosquet 'a grove; thicket'

        brush 'a dense growth of bushes, shrubs, etc.; scrub; thicket'

        bush 'a large uncleared area thickly covered with mixed plant growth, trees, etc., as a jungle'

        carr 'fen; low land that is covered wholly or partly with water unless artificially drained and that usually has peaty alkaline soil and characteristic flora (as of sedges and reeds)'*

        coppice 'a thicket of small trees or bushes; a small wood'

        copse 'a thicket of small trees or bushes; a small wood'

        fen 'low land covered wholly or partially with water; boggy land; a marsh'

        firth 'a long, narrow indentation of the seacoast'

        forest 'a large tract of land covered with trees and underbrush; woodland'

        grove 'a small wood or forested area, usually with no undergrowth'

        heath 'a tract of open and uncultivated land; wasteland overgrown with shrubs'

        holt 'a wood or grove; a wooded hill'

        lea 'a tract of open ground, esp. grassland; meadow'

        moor 'a tract of open, peaty, wasteland, often overgrown with heath, common in high latitudes and altitudes where drainage is poor; heath'

        scrub 'a large area covered with low trees and shrubs'

        shaw 'a small wood or thicket'

        spinney 'a small wood or thicket'

        stand 'the growing trees, or those of a particular species or grade, in a given area'

        thicket 'a thick or dense growth of shrubs, bushes, or small trees; a thick coppice' timberland 'land covered with timber-producing forests'

weald 'wooded or uncultivated country'

wold 'an elevated tract of open country'

woodlot 'a tract, esp. on a farm, set aside for trees'

   c. Answers will vary. An answer supporting the idea that English speakers have a richer concept of woodlands than speakers whose language has fewer words might argue that the plethora of words itself is evidence that the speakers have a rich concept of woodlands. An argument against this might say that a speaker's concept of woodlands probably had more to do with that speaker's personal experience with different types of woodlands, perhaps due to the geography of the area in which he lives, and less to the words available to describe those woodlands in his language. Following this argument, if a group of speakers of a language without many words for woodlands moved to a new area and were suddenly experiencing different types of woodlands on a daily basis and needing to distinguish between the varying types, these people would probably create new words in their language to fill that need, or perhaps "borrow" needed words from a local language.

17. *English* dge *words.* Answers will vary. A sample list of *dge* words follows. Neutral: *edge, wedge, sledge, pledge, budge, fudge,* and *smidgeon.* Unfavorable: *curmudgeon, sludge, hodge-podge,* and *smudge.* Students should discuss the meaning of *budget.* One possible observation is that *budget* is not necessarily unfavorable, although it does consist of limits. For example, if I had a budget of $10,000 for my birthday party, I would find nothing unfavorable about that. Other potentially neutral *dge* words also include limits, like *edge.* Others could potentially have an unfavorable connotation like *wedge, sledge,* and *budge* which suggest a certain amount of force was used. But again, depending on the situation, that may be favorable or unfavorable. For example, *I really wanted to get the book out from under the car's tire but it wouldn't budge* seems negative, but *I've decided to give you $100 and my mind is made up; I won't budge* could be positive. (Use a Google search for "words beginning with" or "words ending in" to see lists of such words: e.g., search for "words ending in dge.")

18. *Euphemisms.* Answers will vary. Below are three possible examples:

    toilet → bathroom → restroom

    arse → butt → bottom / backside

    negro → black → African American

19. *Cratylus Dialogue.* Answers will vary. Those who find that Socrates' point of view was sufficiently well argued to support the thesis that the relationship between form and meaning is indeed arbitrary might point out Hermogenes' argument that "in different cities and countries there are

7

different names for the same things; Hellenes differ from barbarians in their use of names, and the several Hellenic tribes from one another." In other words we can say that objects in the world are called different things in different languages and sometimes even in different dialects of the same language. On the other hand, answers that find that Socrates' point of view was not sufficiently well argued to support the thesis of arbitrariness might point out his summary of Protagoras' argument that "things are not relative to individuals, and all things do not equally belong to all at the same moment and always, they must be supposed to have their own proper and permanent essence: they are not in relation to us, or influenced by us, fluctuating according to our fancy, but they are independent, and maintain to their own essence the relation prescribed by nature." Put another way, this argument says that each item in the world has its own essence, and presumable name, independently of whether humans speaking any particular language call it by that name or not.

20. *Pirahã*. Answers will vary. Linguist Daniel Everett claims that Pirahã violates some of the universal principles hypothesized by linguists (especially Noam Chomsky). In particular he claims in his article in the journal *Current Anthropology*, Volume 46, Number 4, August–October 2005 that Pirahã lacks embedding, and therefore lacks recursion, which Chomsky predicts is a universal of all languages. Everett also claims that Pirahã has a dearth of terms for number, numerals, and quantification, an absence of color terms, an extremely simple pronominal system, no way to mark the perfect tense, and a simple kinship system. He also mentions other non-linguistic features of the culture such as the absence of creation myths, the lack of individual or collective memory of more than two generations past, and the absence of most types of drawing. Everett makes the strong claim that the language of the Pirahã people is such as it is because of the culture of the Pirahã people. He claims his data show "striking evidence for the influence of culture on major grammatical structures, contradicting Newmeyer's (2002:361) assertion . . . that 'there is no hope of correlating a language's gross grammatical properties with socio-cultural facts about its speakers.'" Students should discuss how convincing they find the data and arguments Everett presents and may refer to the fact that Everett 2005 began a debate that is still ongoing. A retort to Everett 2005 by Nevins, Pesetsky, and Rodrigues may be found in the journal *Language*, Volume 85, Number 2, June 2009 and Everett's response to their retort may be found in the same volume.

21. *The lexicon of the English language.* Answers will vary. Those who argue that the lexicon of English should be counted as all the words in English, past and present, may point out that even if a word is no longer in use, it could be brought into use again if it were needed. Furthermore, although the word is no longer used, it still is an English word that has fallen into

disuse, and not, e.g., a French word. Thus, it should be counted as part of the English lexicon. Those who argue instead that the lexicon of English should only be counted as the words currently in use may point out that it would be absurd to count words that are no longer used by any English speaker as part of the English lexicon, and if this faulty methodology were taken to its extreme we may count words from Proto-Indo-European as belonging to the English lexicon! Obviously, that would be ridiculous, but the line must be drawn somewhere. One logical place to draw that line could be that only those words currently used by any native speaker of English should be counted as being part of the (current) English lexicon.

# Chapter 2

1. *Estimating your vocabulary.* Answers to this question will vary depending on student, dictionary, etc. One example:
   a. Count the number of entries on a typical page. They are usually bold-faced.
      *63 entries per page*
   b. Multiply the number of words per page by the number of pages in the dictionary.
      *63 entries × 1330 pages = approximately 83,790 main entries*
   c. Pick four pages in the dictionary at random. Count the number of words on these pages.
      *61 entries + 62 entries + 68 entries + 61 entries = 252 total*
   d. How many of these words do you know?
      *183 words known*
   e. What percentage of the total words on the four pages do you know?
      *approximately 73%*
   f. Multiply the words in the dictionary by the percent you arrived at in (e).
      *I know approximately 61,000 English words.*

2. *English morphemes.*
   a. retro + act + ive
   b. be + friend + ed
   c. tele + vise
   d. margin
   e. en + dear + ment
   f. psych + ology *or* psych + o + logy
   g. un + palat + able
   h. holi + day
   i. grand + mother
   j. morph + em + ic
   k. mis + treat + ment
   l. de + act + iv + at + tion
   m. salt + peter
   n. air + sick + ness

**10**

o. bureau + crat

p. demo + crat

q. aristo + crat

r. pluto + crat

s. demo + crac + y (Note that in this analysis, *-crat* becomes *-crac* before *-y*.)

t. demo + crat + ic

u. demo + crat + ic + al + ly

v. demo + crat + iz + ation

w. demo + crat + ize

x. demo + crat + iz + er

y. demo + crat + iz + ing

z. demo + crat + iz + ed

3. *Identify morphological sequences.*

| **A** | | **B** | |
|---|---|---|---|
| a. | noisy crow | (3) | phrase consisting of adjective plus noun |
| b. | scarecrow | (1) | compound noun |
| c. | the crow | (6) | grammatical morpheme followed by lexical morpheme |
| d. | crowlike | (5) | root morpheme plus derivational suffix |
| e. | crows | (4) | root morpheme plus inflectional suffix |

4. *Identify morphological elements.*

| **A** | | **B** | |
|---|---|---|---|
| a. | terroriz*ed* | (3) | inflectional suffix |
| b. | un*civil*ized | (1) | free root |
| c. | terror*ize* | (4) | derivational suffix |
| d. | *luke*warm | (2) | bound root |
| e. | *im*possible | (6) | derivational prefix |

5. *Zulu morphology.*

**Part One**

a. The morpheme meaning 'singular' is *um-*.

b. The morpheme meaning 'plural' is *aba-*.

c.

| **Zulu** | **English** |
|---|---|
| -fazi | 'married woman' |
| -fani | 'boy' |
| -zali | 'parent' |
| -fundisi | 'teacher' |
| -bazi | 'carver' |
| -limi | 'farmer' |
| -dlali | 'player' |
| -fundi | 'reader' |

Part Two

d. The verbal suffix morpheme is *-a*.

e. The nominal suffix morpheme is *-i*.

f. A noun is formed in Zulu by suffixing the nominal morpheme and prefixing a singular or plural morpheme to the root. Schematically, this is:

noun = number prefix + root + nominal suffix

g. The root morpheme meaning 'read' is *-fund-*.

h. The root morpheme meaning 'carve' is *-baz-*.

6. *Swedish morphology.*

a. *en*

b. *-or* and *-ar*. If the basic noun ends in a vowel (or perhaps more specifically an *a*, we would need more data to differentiate), use *-or* for plurals, e.g., *lampa / lampor, soffa / soffor*. If the basic noun ends in a consonant, use *-ar* for plurals, e.g., *bil / bilar, stol / stolar*.

c. *-n* and *-en*. If the singular noun ends in a vowel (or perhaps more specifically an *a*, we would need more data to differentiate), use *-n* for the definite, e.g., *lampa / lampan , soffa / soffan*. If the singular noun ends in a consonant, use *-en* for the definite, e.g., *bil / bilen, stol / stolen*.

d. *-na*

e. The plural suffix comes before the definite suffix, e.g., *bil-ar-na* 'the cars.'

f. *flickor* 'girls'; *flickan* 'the girl'; *flickorna* 'the girls'

g. *bussar* 'buses'; *bussen* 'the bus'

7. *Cebuano morphology.*

a. The morpheme *-in-* is used to derive a language name from the word for a person from a certain country. Insert the morpheme *-in-* before the first vowel of the word. This has the effect that if the word begins with a consonant, *-in-* will be infixed after the first consonant of the word and if the word begins with a vowel, *in-* will be prefixed before the first vowel of the word.

b. In the case of vowel-initial words, prefixation. In the case of consonant-initial words, infixation.

c. *sinuwid* 'the Swedish language'; *initalo* 'the Italian language'

d. *furanso* 'a Frenchman'; *unagari* 'a Hungarian'

8. *Dutch morphology.*

a. To form an infinitive, add the suffix *-en* to the root. Schematically, this is:

Infinitive = Root + *-en*

b. To form a past participle, circumfix the discontinuous morpheme *ge- . . . -d* around the root. Schematically, this is:

Past Participle = *ge-* + Root + *-d*

9. *Swahili morphology.*

    a. *m-* prefix attached to singular nouns of Class I

       *wa-* prefix attached to plural nouns of Class I

       *a-* prefix attached to verbs when the subject is a singular noun of Class I

       *wa-* prefix attached to verbs when the subject is a plural noun of Class I

       *ki-* prefix attached to singular nouns of Class II

       *vi-* prefix attached to plural nouns of Class II

       *ki-* prefix attached to verbs when the subject is a singular noun of Class II

       *vi-* prefix attached to verbs when the subject is a plural noun of Class II

       *-toto* 'child'

       *-tu* 'person'

       *-su* 'knife'

       *-kapu* 'basket'

       *-fika* 'arrive'

       *-lala* 'sleep'

       *-anguka* 'fall'

       *-me-* present perfect tense

       *-na-* present progressive tense

       *-ta-* future tense

    b. The verb is constructed by stringing together from left to right (1) the verbal prefix indicating the noun class and the number of the subject, (2) the tense, (3) the verbal stem. Schematically, this is:

       Verb = Class prefix + Tense prefix + Verbal stem

    c. (1) 'The child is falling.' = *Mtoto anaanguka.*

       (2) 'The baskets have arrived.' = *Vikapu vimefika.*

       (3) 'The person will fall.' = *Mtu ataanguka.*

10. *Reduplication in Samoan.*

    **Part One**

    a. (1) 'they weave' = *lalaga*

       (2) 'they travel' = *savavali*

       (3) 'he sings' = *pese*

    b. To form a plural verb form, reduplicate (copy) the penultimate (next to the last) consonant-vowel (CV) syllable and insert it before (or after) that syllable. Schematically, this is:

| Singular verb form: | | | | Plural verb form: | | | | | |
|---|---|---|---|---|---|---|---|---|---|
| $C_1$ | $V_1$ | $C_2$ | $V_2$ | $C_1$ | $V_1$ | $C_1$ | $V_1$ | $C_2$ | $V_2$ |
| l | a | g | a | l | a | l | a | g | a |

**Part Two**

1. partial reduplication (with some morpho-phonological changes)
2. 'kind of light' = *tho thong*
3. 'a little shifty' = *khoʔ khul*
4. 'fat' = *luq*
5. 'crazy' = *khot*
6. To form weakened adjectives of this type, reduplicate (copy) the first vowel of the base form and all the consonants before that vowel, then insert this copy before the first consonant of the base. Schematically, this is:

base adjective form:            weakened adjective form:

| $C_1$ | $V_1$ | $C_2$ | $C_3$ | | $C_1$ | $V_1$ | $C_1$ | $V_1$ | $C_2$ | $C_3$ |
|---|---|---|---|---|---|---|---|---|---|---|
| d | a | n | g | | d | a | d | a | n | g |

base adjective form:            weakened adjective form:

| $C_1$ | $C_2$ | $V_1$ | $C_3$ | | $C_1$ | $C_2$ | $V_1$ | $C_1$ | $C_2$ | $V_1$ | $C_3$ |
|---|---|---|---|---|---|---|---|---|---|---|---|
| k | l | o | h | | k | l | o | k | l | o | h |

However, when the first vowel of the base form is *u*, then the copied form of the vowel will be an *o* and a glottal stop will be added after the copied—and changed—vowel. (Note that this gives us evidence that the copy is in fact the prefixed form, whereas with the Samoan example in Part A we had no such evidence). Schematically, this is:

base adjective form:      weakened adjective form:

| $C_1$ | $V_1 = u$ | $C_2$ | | $C_1$ | $V_1 \rightarrow o$ | ʔ | $C_1$ | $V_1$ | $C_2$ |
|---|---|---|---|---|---|---|---|---|---|
| g | u | h | | g | o | ʔ | g | u | h |

11. *Humorous definitions.* Sample answers:

| | |
|---|---|
| *stalemate:* | 'husband or wife no longer interested' The definition results from incorrectly interpreting this word as a compound of *stale* and *mate*, where *stale* means 'no longer fresh' and *mate* is 'a husband or wife.' |
| *effusive:* | 'able to be merged' This word appears to be related to the stem *fuse*, meaning 'merge' and the suffix *-ive*, meaning 'having a tendency, character, or quality' such as 'creative' or 'explosive.' |
| *tenet:* | 'a group of ten singers' This word has been interpreted as a combination of the number *ten* and the suffix *-et*, such as found in words relating to music, e.g., *quartet* and *duet*. |

| | |
|---|---|
| *dermatology:* | 'a study of derms'<br>The word ending *-ology* as in *biology*, meaning 'study of,' has been recognized, but the definer clearly has no idea what *derm* means. |
| *ingenious:* | 'not very smart'<br>Here, the bound morpheme *-genious* has been mistaken for *genius*, meaning 'very smart' and interpreted as meaning 'not very smart' when the negative morpheme *in-* is prefixed. |
| *finesse:* | 'a female fish'<br>The word was interpreted as the noun *fin* 'fish appendage' plus the suffix *-ess(e)* 'female' as in words such as *lioness* or *actress*. |
| *amphibious:* | 'able to lie on both sea and land'<br>*Amphibious* has been correctly used, but the *phib* part of it is humorously interpreted as *fib*, to tell a lie. |
| *deceptionist:* | 'secretary who covers up for his boss'<br>This is a blend of the words *deception* and *receptionist*. |
| *mathemagician:* | 'Bernie Madoff's accountant'<br>A blend of *mathematician* and *magician*, implying that the person in question is good at manipulating numbers to create a false impression. |
| *sexcedrin:* | 'medicine for mate who says, "sorry, I have a headache."'<br>A blend of the word *sex* with the headache medicine *Excedrin*. |
| *testosteroni:* | 'hormonal supplement administered as pasta'<br>A blend of *testosterone* and any one of the pasta words ending in *-roni* such as *macaroni*. |
| *aesthetomino-phen:* | 'medicine to make you look beautiful'<br>A blend of *aesthetics*—having to do with beauty—and *acetominophen*, the analgesic medicine. |
| *histalavista:* | 'say goodbye to those allergies'<br>The Spanish expression *hasta la vista* 'see you later' is influenced by the allergy medicines called *antihistamines*. |

| | |
|---|---|
| *aquapella:* | 'singing in the shower'<br>The "*a ca*" of *a cappella,* 'singing without instrumental accompaniment,' is taken to be *aqua* meaning 'water.' |
| *melancholy:* | 'dog that guards the cantaloupe patch'<br>*-choly* is pronounced "collie" like the breed of dog that guards sheep, and *melan-* is pronounced "melon" of which a cantaloupe is a type, so a "melon-collie" is a guard dog for a type of melon. |
| *plutocrat:* | 'a dog that rules'<br>*-crat* is correctly interpreted as dealing with rule or governance, as in *democrat* and *aristocrat.* However, *pluto-* here has been misinterpreted as the dog, Pluto, from the Disney cartoons. |

12. *Structure of English words.*

a. construal

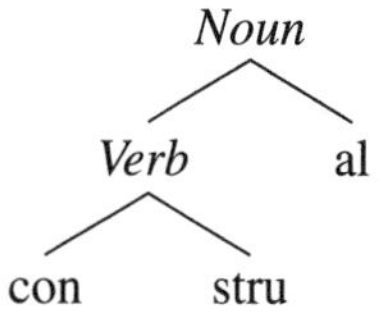


**disappearances**

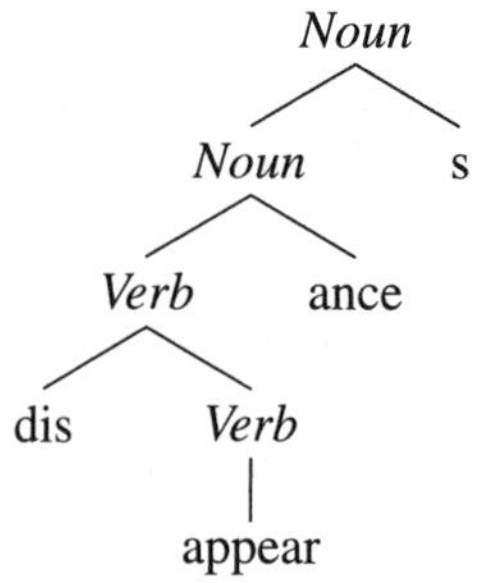


**irreplaceability**

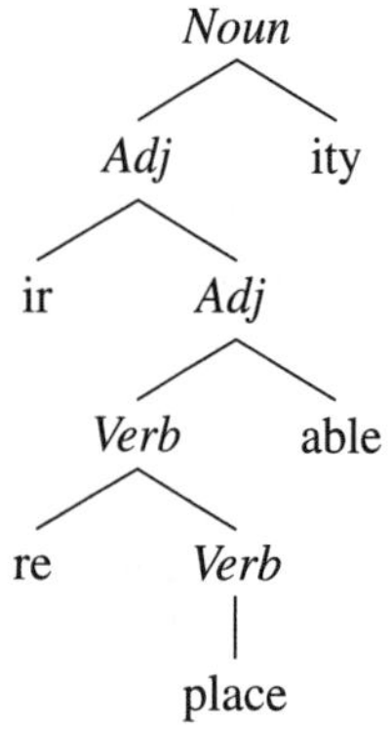


**misconceive**

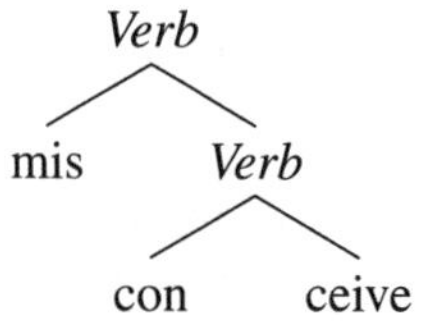

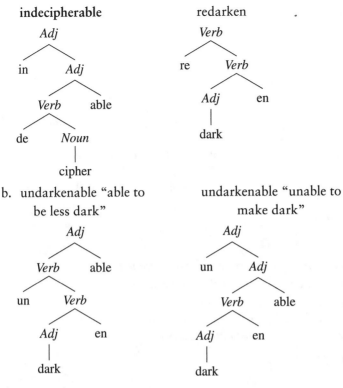

**indecipherable**

Adj
- in
- Adj
  - Verb
    - de
    - Noun
      - cipher
  - able

**redarken**

Verb
- re
- Verb
  - Adj
    - dark
  - en

b. undarkenable "able to be less dark"

Adj
- Verb
  - un
  - Verb
    - Adj
      - dark
    - en
- able

undarkenable "unable to make dark"

Adj
- un
- Adj
  - Verb
    - Adj
      - dark
    - en
  - able

13. *Asymmetries.*

a.

| Words | Nonwords |
|---|---|
| nondescript | *descript |
| incognito | *cognito |
| unbeknownst | *beknownst |
| impeccable | *peccable |
| impromptu | *promptu |
| nonplussed | *plussed |
| indomitable | *domitable |
| misnomer | *nomer |
| democrat | *crat |

b. Answers will vary; examples include *overwhelm* (*whelm*), *cranberry* (*cran*), *inept* (*ept*), *antebellum* (*bellum*), *misgivings* (*givings*), *snowmageddon* (*mageddon*).

14. *Composite words.*

a. Star Trek

b. barnstorm

c. bathrobe

d. ballpoint

e. right-wing

15. *Eight-page book report.*

A report of unspecified
length on a book that is
eight pages long

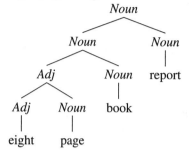

A report that is eight pages long
on a book of unspecified
length

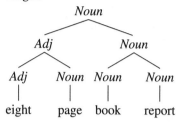

16. *Italian morphology.*

   a. The root morpheme meaning 'robust' is *robust*.
   b. The morpheme meaning 'very' is *-issimo*.
   c. (1) 'a robust wine' = *un vino robusto*
      (2) 'a very red face' = *una faccia rossissima*
      (3) 'a very dry wine' = *un vino seccissimo*

17. *Turkish morphology.*

   a. *-e*
   b. suffixes
   c. 'from an ocean' = *denizden*
   d. three (*deniz-im-de*)

18. *Chickasaw morphology.*

   a. 1. 'to be tall' = *chaaha*
      2. 'to be hungry' = *hopoba*
   b. 1. past tense = *-tok*
      2. 'I' = *sa-*
      3. 'you' = *chi-*
      4. 'he/she' = Ø- (i.e., nothing)
   c. 1. 'you are old' = *chisipokni*
      2. 'he was old' = *sipoknitok*
      3. 'they are old' = *hoosipokni*

19. *Little-End Egglish.*

   i. The possessive morpheme is the prefix *z-*. The first person singular
      morpheme is the suffix *-ego*. The second person morpheme is suffix
      *-ivo*.
   ii. 'my egg white' = *zvelego*

iii. 'hard-boiled egg' = *pe*

iv. 'our' = *-gogo*

v. 'for' = *bo-*

20. *Zoque.*

    a. *-u*

    b. *-pa*

    c. *sohs- / sos-* 'cook'

       *wiht- / wit-* 'walk'

       *sihk- / sik-* 'laugh'

       *kaʔ-* 'die'

       *ken-* 'look'

       *cihc- / cic-* 'tear'

    d. If the verb stem ends with two consonants, the first of those consonants (in this data that is always *h-;* more information would be needed to see whether this is limited to *h* or whether it is true of all consonant clusters in this position), is deleted if the following tense suffix begins with a consonant (in this case, the present tense suffix *-pa*; again, more information would be needed to see whether this applied to other consonant-initial tense suffixes, if there are any). This process seems to function to avoid a sequence of three consonants.

21. *Research exercise.* Answers will vary. A sample answer follows.

    Wictionary.com (accessed in June 2009) lists four English interfixes: *i*, *k*, *n*, and *o* and defines *interfix* as "a vowel inserted interconsonantally betwixt morphemes of Latinate origin in order to ease pronunciation." Note, however, that this definition doesn't work for *k* and *n*, which are not vowels. These four interfixes have three major functions, all of which seem to be different from that of the example given in the book. The *i* and *o* in Wictionary do seem to be used to ease pronunciation, with the *i* being used for words of Latinate origin and the *o* being used for words of Greek origin. The *k* seems to be a purely orthographic "interfix" with examples like *panic/panicky* and *politic/politicking* given. The *n* seems to have yet another use, and is said to be "frequently used with certain suffixes, such as *-ian* and *-ese*, when the base word ends in a vowel that is not readily elided," as in *Javanese* or *Kafkanesque* as opposed to *Kafkaesque* meaning 'resembling the literary work of Franz Kafka.' All of these uses seem true additions of a meaningless morpheme, whereas *jack-i-box* and *man-o-war* seem as though the vowels are potentially reduced forms of a once meaningful word, (*i* being reduced from *in* and *o* being reduced from *of*). Wictionary.com reports that Norwegian also has an interfix, *-e-*.

# Chapter 3

1. *Linguistic knowledge.* Answers will vary.

   a. *Structurally ambiguous sentences.*
      *Example:* I like sweet apples and oranges.
      This sentence is structurally ambiguous because the adjective *sweet* can modify either the noun *apples* or the noun phrase *apples and oranges.* The two structures can be represented in the following ways: (i) I like [[sweet apples] and oranges]—meaning *sweet apples and any kind of oranges.*
      (ii) I like [sweet [apples and oranges]]—meaning *sweet apples and sweet oranges.*

   b. *Sentences with different structures and the same meaning.*
      *Example:* (1) Susie seems to be studying algebra. (2) It seems that Susie is studying algebra.
      These two sentences have different structures but mean the same thing.

   c. *Structurally related sentences.*
      *Example:* (1) I am going to the movies. (2) I am not going to the movies.
      The second sentence can be derived from the first sentence by adding the negative marker *not* after the auxiliary verb *am.* Thus, these two sentences have two different (opposite) meanings and are structurally related.

2. *Infinitely long sentences.*

   A. A possible answer would be: I know that he knows that you know that I hate war.

   B. These sentences show that there is no "longest" sentence in English; one can go on indefinitely, constructing longer and longer sentences by appending "He/she/they/John, etc., know(s) that" to the previously constructed sentence.

   C. While it is true that in principle we could construct a sentence of infinite length (a fact about linguistic competence), in actual behavior there are lapses of memory and mistakes, and we would eventually have to stop constructing a longer sentence in order to eat, drink, and sleep. These are facts about linguistic performance.

3. *Disambiguation with paraphrases.*
   a. Dick finally decided on the boat.
      i. Dick finally chose the boat.
      ii. Dick finally decided (something) when he was on the boat.
   b. The professor's appointment was shocking.
      i. It was shocking that the professor was appointed.
      ii. The appointment made by the professor was shocking.
   c. The design has big squares and circles.
      i. The design has big squares and big circles.
      ii. The design has squares that are big and circles (of unspecified size).
   d. That sheepdog is too hairy to eat.
      i. That sheepdog is too hairy to eat anything.
      ii. That sheepdog is too hairy for someone to eat (the dog).
   e. Could this be the invisible man's hair tonic?
      i. Could this be the hair tonic belonging to the invisible man?
      ii. Could this be the invisible hair tonic for men?
   f. The governor is a dirty street fighter.
      i. The governor fights dirty streets.
      ii. The governor fights unfairly in the streets.
      iii. The governor is a dirty individual who fights in the streets.
   g. I cannot recommend him too highly.
      i. He is superb; nothing I can say would exaggerate his abilities.
      ii. He is mediocre; I cannot recommend him very highly.
   h. Terry loves his wife and so do I.
      i. Terry loves his wife and I love Terry's wife too.
      ii. Terry loves his wife and I love my wife.
   i. They said she would go yesterday.
      i. Yesterday they said, "She will go."
      ii. They said that yesterday was the day she would go.
   j. No smoking section available.
      i. There is no section for smokers.
      ii. A section for nonsmokers is available.
   k. We will dry clean your clothes in 24 hours.
      i. We will dry clean your clothes and they will be ready within 24 hours.
      ii. We will start dry cleaning your clothes 24 hours from now.
   l. I bought cologne for my boyfriend containing 25% alcohol.
      i. For my boyfriend, I bought cologne that consists of 25% alcohol.
      ii. I bought cologne for my boyfriend who (due to drinking too much) consists of 25% alcohol.

4. a. *Baseball joke.* The joke is funny since the catcher intended to say that the batter is a great hitter when it comes to fastballs. The pitcher interpreted the phrase differently, namely that the batter can hit fastballs that are great. This relieved him, since he does not pitch great fastballs. The structural difference can be represented with tree structures as below:

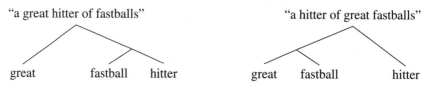

"a great hitter of fastballs"

great      fastball   hitter

"a hitter of great fastballs"

great     fastball      hitter

b. *Advertising exec.* An advertising executive claiming that his magazine has between one and two billion readers may be being honest, but deceptive nonetheless, since the most obvious interpretation of his statement is that his magazine has between one (billion) and two billion readers. But his statement could also mean that his magazine may have only one reader, or any number between the number one and the number two billion. These two structures are represented below:

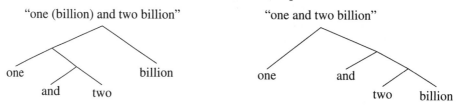

"one (billion) and two billion"

one               billion

and   two

"one and two billion"

one    and

two   billion

## 5. *Representing structural ambiguity.*

The magician touched the child with the wand.
*Meaning 1:* With the wand, the magician touched the child.

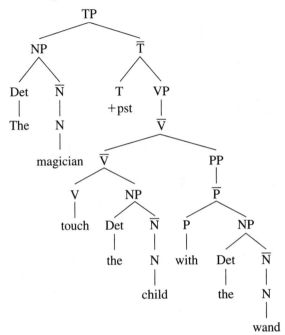

*Meaning 2:* The magician touched the child who has the wand.

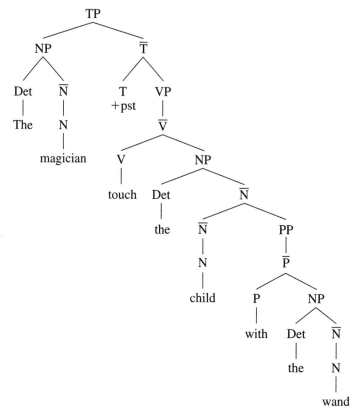

6. *Noun phrase subtrees*

a.

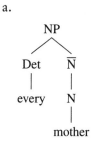

b.

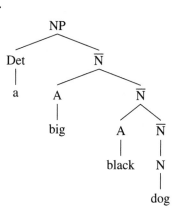

24

c.

d.

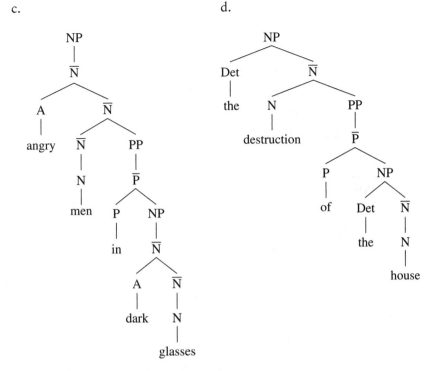

7. *Embedded sentences.*

    a. Yesterday I noticed <u>my accountant repairing the toilet.</u>

    b. Becky said that <u>Jake would play the piano.</u>

    c. I deplore the fact that <u>bats have wings</u>.

    d. That <u>Guinevere loves Lorian</u> is known to all my friends.

    e. Who promised the teacher that <u>Maxine wouldn't be absent</u>?

    f. It's ridiculous that <u>he washes his own Rolls-Royce</u>.

    g. The woman likes for <u>the waiter to bring water when she sits down</u>.

    h. The person <u>who answers this question</u> will win $100.

    i. The idea of <u>Romeo marrying a 13-year-old</u> is upsetting.

    j. I gave my hat to the nurse <u>who helped me cut my hair</u>.

    k. For <u>your children to spend all your royalty payments on recreational drugs</u> is a shame.

    l. Give this fork to the person <u>I'm getting the pie for</u>.

    m. khaw    chyâ    waa    <u>khruu    maa</u>. (Thai)
        he      believe    that    teacher    come
        He believes the teacher is coming.

n. Je me demande quand <u>il partira</u>. (French)
I me ask   when he will leave
I wonder when he'll leave.

o. Jan zei dat <u>Piet dit boek niet heeft gelezen</u>. (Dutch)
Jan said that Piet this book not has read
Jan said that Piet has not read this book.

8. *Phrase structure trees.*

 a. The puppy found the child.

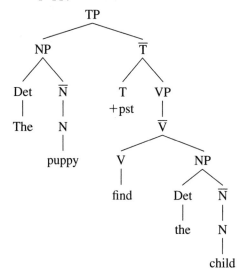

 b. A surly passenger insulted the attendant.

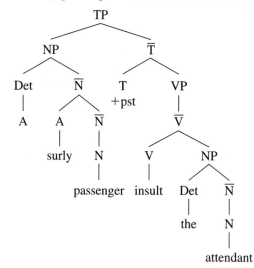

c. The house on the hill collapsed in the earthquake.

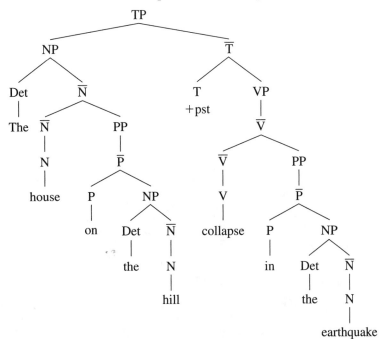

d. The ice melted quickly.

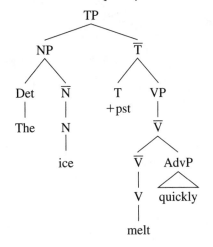

e. The hot sun melted the ice.

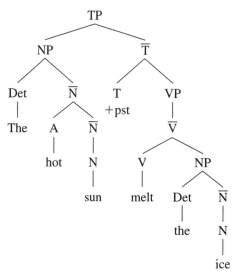

f. The old tree swayed in the wind.

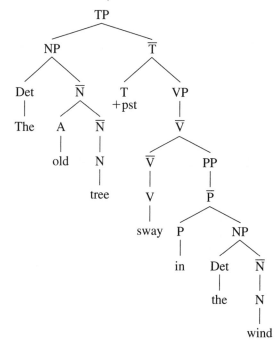

g. My guitar gently weeps.

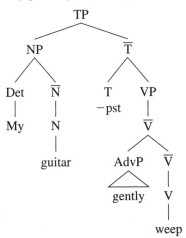

9. *Trees for sentences 6 to 10 words long.* Here are some examples: (Note: We've abbreviated some of the structures illustrated elsewhere with triangles.)

a. The warship sank into the ocean. (6 words)

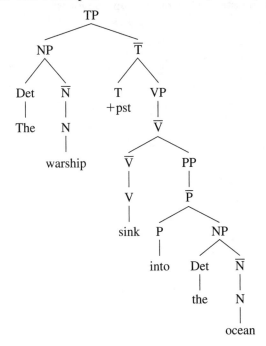

b. The monkey will eat the delicious bananas. (7 words)

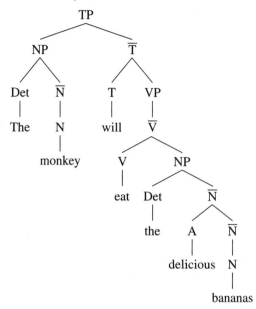

c. The young kids with this strange allergy hiccup. (8 words)

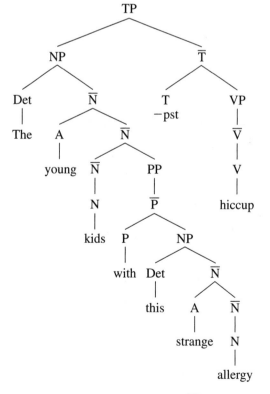

30

d. An otter played in the mud on the bank. (9 words)
   The sentence is structurally ambiguous. This is one possible phrase
   structure tree.

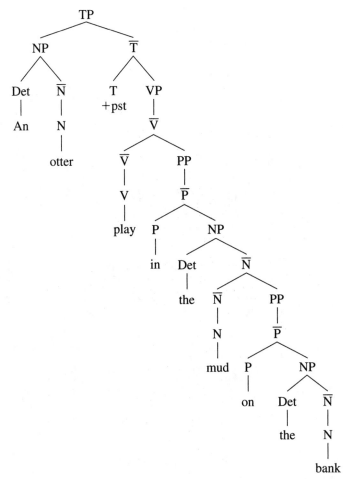

e. The architect found an old picture of the ancient castle. (10 words)

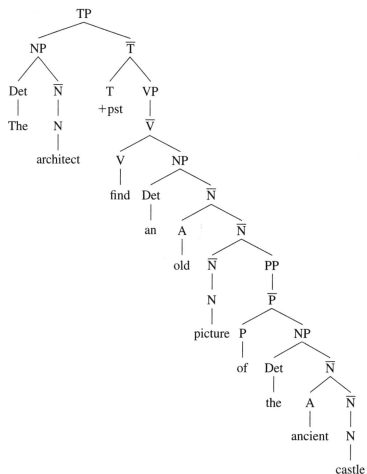

10. *Grammatical sentences.* A grammar that generated all the grammatical sentences plus a few that are not grammatical would not accurately characterize the syntactic knowledge that the speakers of the language have because it would not be able to make distinctions between grammatical and ungrammatical sentences. Since the speaker of the language is able to make such distinctions, this is part of the speaker's knowledge; the grammar in question would not characterize that knowledge.

11. *NP X-bar structures.* Here is one example.

a. *head only*: vase

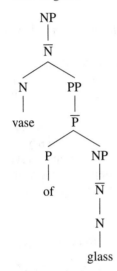

b. *specifier and head only*: the vase

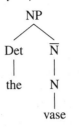

c. *head and complement only*:
   vase of glass

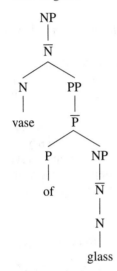

d. *specifier, head, and complement*:
   the vase of glass

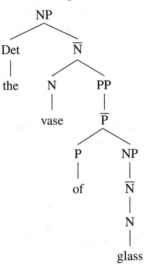

12. *Constituency tests:*

   a. *a lovely pillow*—NP
      Stand-alone test: *What did Martha find for the couch? A lovely pillow.*
      Move as a unit test: *A lovely pillow, Martha found for the couch.*
      Pronoun test: *Martha found it for the couch.*
   b. *light in this room*—not a constituent
      Stand-alone test: *What is terrible? *Light in this room.*
      Move as a unit test: **Light in this room the is terrible.*
      Pronoun test: **The it is terrible.*
   c. *whether Bonnie has finished packing her books*—CP
      Stand-alone test: *What do you wonder? Whether Bonnie has finished packing her books.*

Move as a unit test: *?Whether Bonnie has finished packing her books, I wonder.*

Pronoun test: *I wonder that, too.*

d. *in her class*—PP

Stand-alone test: *Where did Melissa sleep? In her class.*

Move as a unit test: *In her class, Melissa slept.*

Pronoun test: *Melissa slept there.*

e. *Pete and Max*—NP

Stand-alone test: *Who is fighting over the bone? Pete and Max.*

Move as a unit test (with clefting): *It's Pete and Max who are fighting over the bone.*

Pronoun test: *They are fighting over the bone.*

f. *and to Max*—is a constituent

Stand-alone test: *Did you give a bone to Pete, yesterday? Yes, and to Max, too.*

Move as a unit test: *I gave a bone to Pete yesterday and to Max.*

Pronoun test: Does not apply: since *and to Max* is not an NP, we don't expect a pronoun to be able to substitute for it, and since it's not a VP, we don't expect a pro-verbal form to substitute for it.

Another interpretation is that *and to Max* fails this test and perhaps argues against constituency: *\*I gave a bone to Pete him yesterday.* But remember that negative evidence from constituency tests is not as conclusive as positive evidence, since independent grammatical constraints sometimes interfere, leading to false negative results for constituency tests.

g. *Pete and*—not a constituent

Stand-alone test: *\*Who did I give a bone to to Max yesterday? \*Pete and.*

Move as a unit test: *\*Pete and, I gave a bone to to Max yesterday.*

Pronoun test: As with (f) above, either this test does not apply, or it provides negative evidence: *\*I gave a bone to him to Max yesterday.*

13. *Verbal particles.*

a. To show that *up* forms a constituent with the verb in *run up the bill*, we show that nothing can come between them: for example, an adverb like *completely*. This explains the contrast between the grammatical sentence *John ran completely (all the way/right/part way) up the hill*, in which *run* and *up* are not a constituent, and the ungrammatical *\*John ran completely (all the way/right/part way) up the bill.*

b. Only constituents coordinate, so since *up the hill* and *over the bridge* coordinate grammatically in sentence (i), they must be constituents; likewise for *ran up the bill* and *ran off his mouth* in (iii). In contrast, the fact that *up the bill* and *off his mouth* do not coordinate grammatically in sentence (ii) establishes that they are not constituents.

14. *C-selection restrictions.*

    a. *\*The man located.* The verb *locate* is transitive: it requires an NP object.

    b. *\*Jesus wept the apostles.* The verb *weep* is intransitive: it does not allow an object.

    c. *\*Robert is hopeful of his children.* The adjective *hopeful* allows a sentential complement (e.g., *that his children will succeed*) or no complement, but it cannot take a PP complement with *of*.

    d. *\*Robert is fond that his children love animals.* The adjective *fond* allows a PP complement with *of*, but cannot take a sentential complement.

    e. *\*The children laughed the man.* Like *weep*, the verb *laugh* is intransitive and may not take a direct object.

15. *Ditransitive verbs.* Sample answers:

    (1) *bring:* The vassal brought the emperor a gift.

    (2) *throw:* The pitcher threw Sam the ball.

    (3) *send:* I sent Mary a letter.

16. *Tamil.*

    i. Head final. These prepositional phrases all end with a preposition.

    ii.

17. *Tamil VPs and NPs.* The data further support the hypothesis in 16 that Tamil is head final. The data shows head final VPs: *a story tell* where *tell* is the head V and it follows its complement *a story* and *a cow sell* where the head V *sell* follows the complement *a cow*. The VP structure in Tamil is:

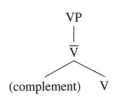

We are also given data on NPs in Tamil: *a story, the boy, a cow,* and *woman this.* If we treat *this* as a determiner, then we must say that some determiner can appear to the right of the noun in Tamil, perhaps demonstrative determiners. This isn't a counter-example to the head-final-ness of Tamil, however, since that specification has to do with the head and its complement, not a head and its specifier. We have no examples of

35

complements to nouns in Tamil, so we cannot say whether NPs are head initial or head final in Tamil. The two possible structures we have for NPs in Tamil are:

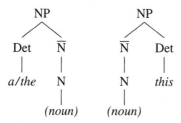

18. Wh- *movement*. Sample answers:

a.

*what*

    i.  What would the child like?

    ii.  d-structure: The child would like what?

*which*

    i.  Which color has Percy decided on?

    ii.  d-structure: Percy has decided on which color?

*where*

    i.  Where is Marcy going for her vacation?

    ii.  d-structure: Marcy is going where for her vacation?

a. *Sample answer:*

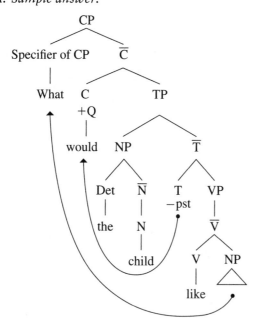

36

19. *Ditransitive verbs.*

    a. The relationship between the two NPs following the verb in the pairs of sentences is regular. (1) The NP object of the preposition in the second sentence of each pair corresponds to the NP object immediately to the right of the verb in the first sentence of each pair. (Labeled $NP_1$ in the schema below.) (2) The NP object immediately to the right of the verb in the second sentence of each pair corresponds to the second NP object after the verb in the first sentence. (Labeled $NP_2$ in the schema below.) Schematically this is:

        Sentence 1: Subject Verb $NP_1$ $NP_2$
        Sentence 2: Subject Verb $NP_2$ to $NP_1$

    b. It is possible to derive one of these structures from the other because the relationships between the two types of sentences are structure-dependent and systematic. Either one could be derived from the other—linguists disagree as to which sentence is closest to d-structure. If the first sentence is derived from the second sentence, then *to* is deleted and its object ($NP_1$/*the senator*/*the Animal Rights Movement*) is moved to the immediate right of the verb. If the second sentence is derived from the first sentence, the second NP of the first sentence ($NP_2$/*a letter*/*$1,000,000*) is moved to the immediate right of the verb and *to* is inserted in front of what is now the second NP ($NP_1$/*the senator*/*the Animal Rights Movement*).

20. *Cross-linguistic syntactic variation.* Sample answers:

    a. *French:*

        i. French marks future tense on the main verb, while English requires an auxiliary verb to mark the future.

        ii. In French, the adjective follows the noun it modifies, while in English the adjective precedes the noun it modifies.

        iii. In French, the adjective agrees in number with the noun it modifies, while in English it does not.

        iv. In French, the definite article agrees in number with the noun it precedes, while in English it does not.

    b. *Japanese:*

        i. Japanese has subject markers and object markers, which indicate grammatical relations in all noun phrases (nominal and pronominal), while English does not.

        ii. In Japanese, the verb follows the object, while in English the object follows the verb.

        iii. In Japanese, the auxiliary *iru* follows the main verb, while in English auxiliaries always precede the main verb.

c. *Swahili:*

  i.   Swahili has class markers. These are prefixes that distinguish various classes of nouns and indicate whether they are singular or plural. English has only plural suffixes.

  ii.  Swahili verbs are marked for present and past tense with a prefix. English verbs are marked for tense with a suffix or with auxiliary verbs.

  iii. Swahili verbs (both in the past and present tenses) have prefixes agreeing in number (and class) with the subject. English regular verbs agree in number only in the present tense with a third-person singular subject; the agreement is marked by one suffix (-s).

d. *Korean:*

  i.   Korean (like Japanese) has suffixes on all noun phrases indicating grammatical relations like subject and object, while in English the distinction only surfaces in pronouns.

  ii.  Korean has verb suffixes that indicate whether the sentence is an assertion or a question. English has no such suffixes.

  iii. In a *wh* question in Korean, the *wh* phrase does not move to the beginning of the sentence, while in English it does.

  iv.  In Korean (like Japanese), the verb follows the object, while in English the verb precedes the object.

  v.   Korean does not use auxiliary verbs to form questions, while English does.

e. *Tagalog:*

  i.   In Tagalog, proper names like Pedro occur with articles, while in English they cannot.

  ii.  In Tagalog, the verb precedes the subject, while in English the subject precedes the verb.

  iii. In Tagalog, there are topic markers, while in English topics are not marked overtly.

  iv.  In Tagalog, the complementizer (-*ng*) introducing an embedded clause is a nominal suffix on the subject of the main clause. In English, the complementizer (*that*) is a free morpheme that precedes the subject of an embedded clause.

21. *Transformationally induced ambiguity.*

    The sentence *Do you still love me as much as you used to?* with the meaning as intended by the husband is derived from:

    *Do you still love me as much as you used to [love me]?*

The following underlying structures are also possible (though less likely):

*Do you still love me as much as you used to [love Mary/ice cream/ skiing]?*
*Do you still love me as much as you used to [sit in chairs/read books]?*

In this way, many possible underlying forms are transformed into a single surface structure, making it ambiguous.

22. *Adverbs in French and English.*

a. In French, adverbs of frequency must follow the verb, whereas in English, they must precede the verb.

b. If adverbs of frequency originate left adjoined to $\overline{V}$ and do not move, then in order for the adverb to end up after the verb in French, the verb must move to a position in front of (higher than) the adverb. The additional grammatical sentence helps us hypothesize where the verb moves to:

*Jean a toujours bu du vin.*
Jean has always drunk wine
'Jean has always drunk wine.'

In the sentence *Jean a toujours bu du vin* we see that if T is already occupied by an overt lexical item, like the auxiliary verb *a* 'has', then it blocks the verb from moving into that position. Notice <u>in</u> both the PS trees below, the AdvP *toujours* originates left adjoined to $\overline{V}$ and remains there. In the case with no overt auxiliary verb (on the left), the verb raises to T giving the order S-V-Adv-O. In the case with an overt auxiliary verb (on the right), the verb cannot raise to T, as it is already filled, and we get the order S-Aux-Adv-V-O.

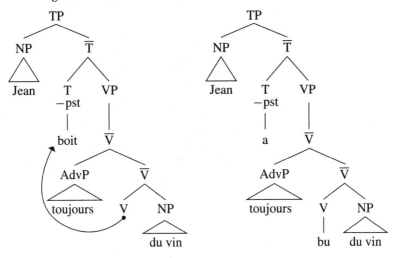

c. English and French are the same in terms of the d-structure. In both English and French, the adverb of frequency originates in the same place, as does the verb, the tense, and the subject and object. Where English and French differ is that French raises main verbs to T as long as there is no lexical item (e.g., an aux verb) there. English, however, appears to leave main verbs in V, as seen in the trees below:

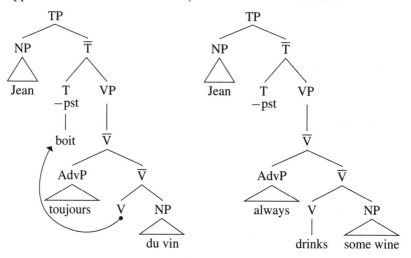

23. *Modifiers.*

a. It must be the case that the NP comes before the AdvP, as we can see if we use substitution with a different NP and AdvP: *cursed him yesterday* but *\*cursed yesterday him.*

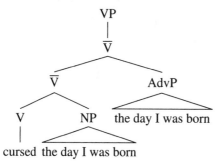

b. The rule $\overline{N} \rightarrow A\ \overline{N}$ could be modified to $\overline{N} \rightarrow AP\ \overline{N}$. This would allow adjectival phrases to modify nouns. These adjectival phrases could themselves be complex, with intensifiers or with PP complements, for example. The rule is still recursive, so multiple such adjective phrases would be allowed, as in *the extremely intelligent, happy-about-his-grade boy* as shown below:

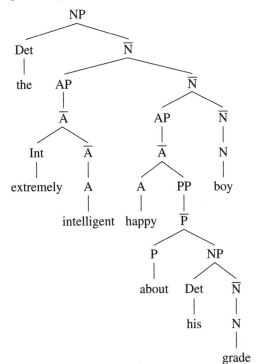

24. *Embedded CPs.* Answers will vary. The following data support the constituency of the underlined CPs.

> *Stand alone:* What did Sam ask? <u>If he could play soccer.</u>
> *Move as a unit (with clefting):* <u>Whether Michael walked the dog</u> is what I wonder.
> *Pronoun replacement test:* Cher believes <u>it.</u>
> *Move as a unit (with clefting):* <u>That the students know the answer</u> is what Cher believes.
> *Move as a unit:* <u>That Sam broke his arm</u> is a problem.

## 25. Complementizer deletion.

a.

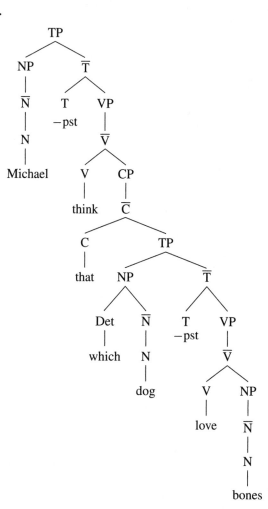

b.

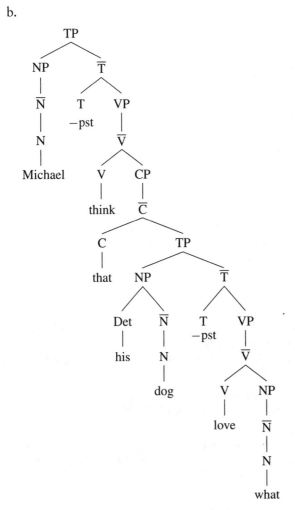

c. *That*-deletion is obligatory from the C position when the TP that is sister to that C lacks a subject (e.g., in the case where the subject has been moved); otherwise it is optional.

26. *Dutch and German questions.* The data show that Dutch and German questions are different from English questions in that *do*-insertion is not used either for *wh* questions that question the subject (ii) nor for yes/no questions (iii). It appears that Dutch and German do not use the *do*-insertion strategy at all.

27. *Challenge research exercise: ditransitive verbs in X-bar theory.* There are several proposals for handling ditransitive verbs in X-bar theory, most of which involve positing additional structure above the VP. One common realization of this hypothesis is known as "little-v", or "vP shells."

(Note that the *v* here is intentionally lower case.) The vP is posited to be a level above the VP; every VP (ditransitive or not) has a projecting vP. For ditransitive verbs, both objects originate in the lowest VP: one as the complement to the V and one in the specifier position to V. The verb then raises from V to v, as shown below:

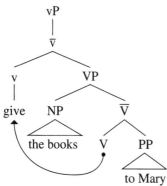

28. One-*replacement test.*

a. *with the golden arm* = adjunct
    The man with the golden arm and the one with the bionic leg . . .

b. *for proposition eighteen* = adjunct
    A voter for proposition eighteen and one against were both interviewed by the news.

c. *at his home* = complement
    *My cousin's arrival at his home and the one at his office surprised everyone.

d. *of a retaining wall* = complement
    *The construction of a retaining wall and the one of the guest house were both expensive.

e. *in the river* = adjunct
    The boat in the river and the one at the dock are both brand new.

f. *white with foam* = adjunct
    There are three oceans on this planet: the ocean white with foam and the one red with blood are the largest.

g. *of the temple* = complement
    *The desecration of the temple and the one of the sanctuary were especially abhorrent.

h. *of Julius Caesar* = complement
    *The betrayal of Julius Caesar and the one of Jesus Christ are both well known.

# Chapter 4

1. *Compositional semantics.*

   **A.** i, iii

   **B.** i.   the set consisting of Anna

   ii.  the set consisting of Paul and Benjamin

   iii. the set consisting of nothing (the *empty set*)

   **C.** i, iii

   **D. Challenge exercise.**

   a.   Since nobody kissed Laura, the meaning of *kissed* contains no pairs of individuals whose second member is (the individual) Laura. Thus, Semantic Rule II determines that the meaning of *kissed Laura* is the set consisting of no individuals (the empty set); Semantic Rule I determines that the sentence *Jack kissed Laura* is true if (the individual) Jack is a member of this set, and false otherwise. Since Jack is not a member of the set containing no individuals, the semantic rules correctly determine that the sentence is false.

   b.   Since Jack did not kiss Laura, the meaning of *kissed* does not contain the pair <Jack, Laura>. Thus, Semantic Rule II determines that the meaning of *kissed Laura* is a set that does not contain (the individual) Jack, though it will contain other men (since others did kiss Laura). Semantic Rule I determines that the sentence *Jack kissed Laura* is true if (the individual) Jack is a member of this set, and false otherwise, so the semantic rules correctly determine the sentence to be false.

2. *Truth (falsity) in virtue of meaning vs. truth dependent on the facts.*

   a. T

   b. C

   c. S

   d. S

   e. S

   f. C

   g. S

   h. T

   i. S

**45**

j. S
k. T
l. S
m. S
n. T
o. C
p. S
q. C
r. C
s. C
t. S
u. C
v. S
w. C
x. C
y. S
z. C

3. *Homonyms.* The pairs of words *flour* and *flower* are homonyms, i.e., they sound the same but are different words (or morphemes) since they have different meanings. *Flour* and *flower* are also spelled differently, but that is not a requirement of a homonym. The pair *ground* and *ground* in the passage are also homonyms.

4. *What a speaker means.* No. There are many facets of "meaning" that, while related to the meanings of words and the way they are put together (*linguistic meaning*), are not strictly part of this linguistic meaning. An example is the word *or.* Suppose that you ask your mother where your jacket is, and she responds, "It's in the closet or hanging in the hallway." You'll naturally understand—the information will be conveyed—that she doesn't know in which of these places it is. This isn't strictly part of the meaning of the word *or* (the most likely candidate in the sentence), how-ever, as we can see if we change the situation slightly. Suppose now that you're playing a game with your sister, who has hidden your jacket, and you have to find it. You ask the same question and get the same answer; you will certainly not understand the she doesn't know where it is (and hence this can't be part of the linguistic meaning, since she said exactly the same words your mother did). In the first case, this "extra" informa-tion is something inferred from what your mother said and the particular context. The job of semantics is to characterize those aspects of meaning determined by the words and the way they are put together, which hold constant across all uses (for a given language community).

5. *Ambiguity; paraphrases.*

   **Part One**

   a. We laughed at the colorful ball.
      i.   At the colorful dance, we laughed.
      ii.  We found the colorful dance amusing.
      iii. We found the colorful toy amusing.

   b. He was knocked over by the punch.
      i.   He was intoxicated by the fruit drink.
      ii.  He was physically knocked over due to intoxication by the fruit drink.
      iii. He was physically knocked over by the punch bowl.
      iv.  He was knocked over by a punch from someone's fist.
      v.   He was impressed by the (taste) of the fruit drink.
      vi.  He was impressed by the physical punch someone (perhaps a boxer) gave to someone else.

   c. The police were urged to stop drinking by the fifth.
      i.   The police were urged to quit drinking whole fifths of liquor.
      ii.  The police were urged to quit drinking alcohol by the fifth of the month.
      iii. The police were urged to stop people from drinking whole fifths of liquor.
      iv.  The police were urged to stop people from drinking liquor by the fifth of the month.

   d. I said I would file it on Thursday.
      i.   It was Thursday when I said I would put it in the file drawer.
      ii.  It was Thursday when I said I would file it using a rasp.
      iii. I said that Thursday I would put it in the file drawer.
      iv.  I said that Thursday I would file it down using a rasp.

   e. I cannot recommend visiting professors too highly.
      i.   I strongly recommend that you visit professors.
      ii.  I do not recommend that you visit professors.
      iii. I strongly recommend professors who are visiting.
      iv.  I do not recommend professors who are visiting.

   f. The license fee for pets owned by senior citizens who have not been altered is $1.50. (Actual notice)
      i.   The license fee for pets owned by unaltered senior citizens is $1.50.
      ii.  The license fee for unaltered pets owned by senior citizens is $1.50.

g. What looks better on a handsome man than a tux? Nothing! (Attributed to Mae West)
    i. A handsome man looks better when he's wearing a tux than when he's wearing anything else.
    ii. A handsome man looks better when he's wearing nothing than when he's wearing a tux.
h. Wanted: Man to take care of cow that does not smoke or drink. (Actual notice)
    i. Wanted: Man who does not smoke or drink to take care of cow.
    ii. Wanted: Man to take care of a nonsmoking, nondrinking cow.
i. For Sale: Several old dresses from grandmother in beautiful condition. (Actual notice)
    i. For Sale: Several old dresses in beautiful condition from grandmother.
    ii. For Sale: Several old dresses from grandmother, who is in beautiful condition.
j. Time flies like an arrow.
    i. Time proceeds as quickly as an arrow proceeds.
    ii. Measure the speed of flies in the same way that you measure the speed of an arrow.
    iii. Measure the speed of flies in the same way that an arrow measures the speed of flies.
    iv. Measure the speed of flies that are similar to an arrow.
    v. Flies of a particular kind, namely time-flies, are fond of an arrow.

**Part Two**
a. POLICE BEGIN CAMPAIGN TO RUN DOWN JAYWALKERS
    i. Police begin campaign to systemically clamp down on jaywalking.
    ii. Police begin campaign to run over jaywalkers with squad cars.
b. DRUNK GETS NINE MONTHS IN VIOLIN CASE
    i. Drunk sentenced to nine months for his involvement in violin case.
    ii. Drunk sentenced to spend nine months imprisoned in a violin case.
c. FARMER BILL DIES IN HOUSE
    i. A farmer, Bill, dies in (his) house.
    ii. A bill pertaining to farmers fails to be enacted by the House of Representatives.
d. STUD TIRES OUT
    i. Stores are sold out of studded tires.
    ii. A stud is running low on energy.
    iii. Studded tires have gone out of fashion.
e. SQUAD HELPS DOG BITE VICTIM
    i. A victim of a dog bite is helped by a squad.
    ii. A squad helps a dog bite its victim.

f. LACK OF BRAINS HINDERS RESEARCH
  i.   Research on brains is compromised by lack of samples.
  ii.  Someone's stupidity is hindering research.

g. MINERS REFUSE TO WORK AFTER DEATH
  i.   Miners strike because of someone's death.
  ii.  Miners proclaim that they won't work when dead/dead miners refuse to work.

h. EYE DROPS OFF SHELF
  i.   Eye drops are sold out.
  ii.  An eye falls off a shelf.
  iii. Eye drops were withdrawn by the manufacturer.

i. JUVENILE COURT TO TRY SHOOTING DEFENDANT
  i.   Court that tries juveniles/court comprised of juveniles is slated to bring defendant to trial in shooting case.
  ii.  Court that tries juveniles/court comprised of juveniles will experiment with shooting defendant (as a punishment).

j. QUEEN MARY HAVING BOTTOM SCRAPED
  i.   The ship Queen Mary is having its underside cleaned of buildup.
  ii.  The Queen, Mary, is having her bottom scraped (!).

6. *Ambiguities.*

  a. He waited by the bank.
    i.   He waited by the financial building.
    ii.  He waited by the shore.

  b. Is he really that kind?
    i.   Is he really that type?
    ii.  Is he really that compassionate?

  c. The proprietor of the fish store was the sole owner.
    i.   The proprietor of the fish store owned the flatfish.
    ii.  The proprietor of the fish store was the only owner.

  d. The long drill was boring.
    i.   The lengthy tool was drilling a hole.
    ii.  The lengthy tool was not interesting.
    iii. The long exercise was dull.
    iv.  The long exercise (in woodworking class) was drilling a hole.

  e. When he got the clear title to the land, it was a good deed.
    i.   It was good of him to get the title to the land.
    ii.  The clear title to the land was valid.

  f. It takes a good ruler to make a straight line.
    i.   It takes a good straightedge to make a straight line.
    ii.  It takes a good monarch to make a straight line.

**49**

g. He saw that gasoline can explode.
  i. He watched as that can of gasoline exploded.
  ii. He understood that it's possible for gasoline to explode.
h. You should see her shop.
  i. You should see the way she shops.
  ii. You should see the shop that she owns.
i. Every man loves a woman.
  i. For every man, there is a woman whom he loves.
  ii. There is one woman who is loved by every man.
j. You get half off the cost of your hotel room if you make your own bed.
  i. You get half off the cost of your room if you physically build the piece of furniture, the bed.
  ii. You get half off the cost of your room if you put your sheets in order on the bed yourself.
k. "It's his job to lose," (said the coach about the new player).
  i. He is so secure in his job that he would have to go out of his way to lose his job.
  ii. It's a requirement of the player's job that he loses.
l. "We will change your oil in 10 minutes" (sign in front of a garage).
  i. We will begin your oil change 10 minutes from now.
  ii. It will take us 10 minutes to change your oil, once we start.
m. **Challenge exercise:** Bill wants to marry a Norwegian woman.
  i. There is a particular woman who Bill wants to marry, who is Norwegian.
  ii. Bill wants to marry a Norwegian woman, but he doesn't have any particular one in mind. Maybe he just likes Norwegian women.

7. *Idioms.* Answer here will vary. Sample answers:
  a. They tied the knot.
  b. Go suck an egg.
  c. She called him every name in the book.
  d. Let's call it a day.
  e. He's a real kick in the pants.
  f. Shake a leg!

8. *Etymology of idioms.* Students should try to research the etymology of their idioms, but are free to speculate as well. Answers will vary. Sample answers:
  a. *They tied the knot.* According to the webpage www.phrases.org.uk /meanings/tie-the-knot.html, ". . . this expression derives from the nets of knotted string which supported beds prior to the introduction

**50**

of metal-sprung bedframes. The theory goes that in order to make a marriage bed, you needed to 'tie the knot'." However, the page goes on to say that, "there's not a shred of evidence to support this idea." The page points out that the association of knots with marriage could either be literal, since tying knots is actually part of some marriage ceremonies, or it could be metaphorical, in which case, "the knot is merely symbolic of a lasting unity."

b. *Go suck an egg.* A blogger on the webpage www.phrases.org.uk /bulletin_board/44/messages/45.html uses the *Oxford English Dictionary* (*OED*) to support a theory about the origin of the phrase *Go suck an egg.* He notes that

> The OED2 . . . record[s] an obsolete term *to suck the eggs of* meaning "to extract the goodness of, cause to be unproductive" . . . In addition, we have the noun *suck-egg*, with the following senses: "a. An animal that is reputed to suck eggs, e.g., a weasel, cuckoo; fig. an avaricious person; b. A young fellow; slang. a silly person (Barre & Leland); . . . Also U.S. dial. (chiefly South and Midland), used to designate a dog regarded as the type of viciousness or worthlessness.

The blogger sums up by saying that, "All in all, these seem to add up to a sense of 'sucking eggs' as a dishonest, contemptible, or foolish activity."

c. *She called him every name in the book.* We couldn't find any information about this online, but it seems like it might come from the idea that there is a book full of all the bad names one might call someone, a book of insults, if you will. And that if you're really ticked off at someone, you might just start at the beginning of that book and call the offending party every name in the book. (Also, see insults in the style of Shakespeare in the computational syntax section on pp. 503–505).

d. *Let's call it a day.* Again, we couldn't find anything definitive online. Perhaps this is related to a sports analogy where a game can be called over (ended) by an umpire or other type of referee. In analogy to an outside judge making calls regarding when the game will end, the person saying "let's call it a day," is saying "let's judge some activity to be over for now, whether it is or not, and whether the day is over or not."

e. *He's a real kick in the pants.* According to www.yourdictionary.com /idioms/kick-in-the-pants-a, *kick in the pants* can be either a compliment meaning something exciting or an insult meaning something humiliating or a rebuff. We couldn't find anything that spoke directly to the origin of the phrase. We can see why getting kicked in the pants, i.e., the buttocks, might be a negative thing, but it's less obvious why it might be positive. Perhaps the positive meaning comes from getting kicked in the pants being something unexpected and surprising, that wakes you up and makes you take notice.

f. *Shake a leg!* This means 'hurry up' and according to www.phrases.org.uk
/meanings/shake-a-leg.html, comes from the idea of "rous[ing] yourself
from sleep and getting out of bed," which perhaps involves shaking a
leg that has "fallen asleep" as you slept.

9. *Semantic properties.*

  a. The (a) and (b) words are **male animate**.
    The (a) words are **human**.
    The (b) words are **nonhuman**.

  b. The (a) words are **countable (count nouns)**.
    The (b) words are **uncountable (mass nouns)**.

  c. The (a) words are **concrete**.
    The (b) words are **abstract**.

  d. The (a) and (b) words are **plants**.
    The (a) words are **trees**.
    The (b) words are **flowers**.

  e. The (a) words are things that are **written**.
    The (b) words are **things to write with (writing implements)**.

  f. The (a) and (b) words are **motion verbs**.
    The (a) words are **motions of the body (without a vehicle)**.
    The (b) words are **motions with a vehicle**.

  g. The (a) and (b) words are verbs of **speaking**.
    The (a) words **do not indicate manner of speaking**.
    The (b) words **do indicate manner of speaking**.

  h. The (a) and (b) words are **adjectives that show antonymy**.
    The (a) words are **complementary pairs of antonyms**.
    The (b) words are **gradable pairs of antonyms**.

  i. The (a) words are **non-implicational adjectives** (an alleged murderer is
    not necessarily a murderer).

    The (b) words are **implicational adjectives** (a stupid murderer is neces-
    sarily a murderer). *Note*: the term *implicational* is not standard for this
    distinction. It is important only to understand what the distinction is,
    namely, that it follows from *x is an ADJ N* that *x is an N* for the adjec-
    tives in (b) but not *necessarily* for the type of adjectives in (a).

10. "*-nym.*" Answers will vary. Sample answers:

According to Wiktionary.org, *-onym* comes from the Ancient Greek
*onuma*, which is the Doric dialectal form of *onoma*, meaning 'name'.
We see this in the common English word *synonym* and the not-so-common
English word *euonym*, which was the winning word in the 1997 Scripps
National Spelling Bee.

Below are a few more -*nym* words:

1. meronym: a part of a whole. *Wheel* is a meronym of *bicycle*.
2. pseudonym: a fictitious name. *George Orwell* is a pseudonym of Eric Blair.
3. anonym: one who conceals his true name.
4. mononym: a name consisting of a single word. *Tati*, a French actor.
5. eponym: a place, period, people, etc., named after a person: for example, *spoonerism* after the Reverend William A. Spooner, warden of New College, Oxford.
6. autonym: a word that describes itself. *Noun* is an autonym because it is a noun.
7. tautonym: a reduplicative word such as *beri-beri*.
8. patronym: a family name based on the name of the father, such as *Richardson*, son of Richard.
9. contronym: this is a synonym of autoantonym, which is a word with several meanings, one of which is defined as the opposite of one of its other meanings, like *overlook*, which can mean 'to watch, inspect' and 'to forget'.
10. exonym: the name of a place used by foreigners when different from the native name, such as *Japan* for Nippon or *Rome* for Roma.

11. *Complementary, gradable, and relational opposites.*

| A | B | C |
|---|---|---|
| good | bad | g |
| expensive | cheap | g |
| parent | offspring | r |
| beautiful | ugly | g |
| false | true | c |
| lessor | lessee | r |
| pass | fail | c |
| hot | cold | g |
| legal | illegal | c |
| larger | smaller | r |
| poor | rich | g |
| fast | slow | g |
| asleep | awake | c |
| husband | wife | r |
| rude | polite | g |

12. *Homonyms.*

| | | | |
|---|---|---|---|
| a. "Naked": | bare | bear | |
| b. "Base metal": | lead | led | |
| c. "Worships": | prays | praise | preys |
| d. "Eight bits": | byte | bite | bight |
| e. "One of five senses": | sight | site | cite |

53

f. "Several couples": pairs pares pears
g. "Not pretty": plain plane
h. "Purity of gold unit": karat carrot caret
i. "A horse's coiffure": mane main Maine
j. "Sets loose": frees freeze frieze

13. *Proper name puns.*

   a. Custer's last stand

   b. enchiladas

   c. ptomaine (commonly known as food poisoning)

   d. lying on the beach

   e. winner takes all

   f. Peter, Paul, and Mary

   g. thanks for the memories

   h. dressed to kill

   i. dearly beloved

   j. *Gone with the Wind*

   k. anchovy pizza

   l. polyester

   m. grapevine

   n. tie me up

   o. *Romancing the Stone*

   p. brouhaha

   q. see you later

   r. discotheque

   s. thanks a lot

   t. nincompoop

   u. Viagra

14. *Thematic relations.*

   a     t
   a. Mary found a ball.

    a         s        g
   b. The children ran from the playground to the wading pool.

      a        t       i
   c. One of the men unlocked all the doors with a paper clip.

    a     t     i
   d. John melted the ice with a blowtorch.

    a        t
   e. Helen looked for a cockroach.

     e             t

  f. Helen saw a cockroach.

       a

  g. Helen screamed.

         t

  h. The ice melted.

           i        e          t

  i. With a telescope, the boy saw the man.

         a         t          g

  j. The farmer loaded hay onto the truck.

         a         t          i

  k. The farmer loaded the hay with a pitchfork.

     t             g           a

  l. The hay was loaded on the truck by the farmer.

     e             t                s

  m. Helen heard the music coming out of the speaker.

15. *The Jabberwocky.*

    a. *gyre*: v. to move in a circle or spiral; n. a circular or spiral motion or form, especially a giant circular oceanic surface current.

    b. *mome*: n. blockhead, fool.

    c. *jabberwocky*: n. meaningless speech or writing (origin is from *Jabberwocky* itself).

    d. *whiffle*: v. 1. a. of the wind: to blow unsteadily or in gusts. b. vacillate. 2. to emit or produce a light whistling or puffing sound.

    e. *burble*: v. 1. bubble. 2. babble, prattle.

    f. *galumph*: vi. to move with a clumsy heavy tread.

    g. *beamish*: adj. beaming and bright with optimism, promise, or achievement.

    h. *chortle*: vi. 1. to sing or chant exultantly. 2. to laugh or chuckle esp. in satisfaction or exultation (origin is also from *Jabberwocky*).

16. *Performatives.* Answers will vary. Samples:

    a. In a game of tag, someone becomes "it" when the person who is currently "it" touches him/her and shouts, "You're it!"

    b. A person becomes a knight when the queen says, "I dub thee Sir Rodney."

    c. In Scrabble, you can challenge the validity of a word by saying, "I challenge."

    d. Two people are married when the preacher says, "I hereby pronounce you husband and wife."

    e. In card games like pinochle, the bidding is opened when the dealer says, "The bid is open."

17. *Performance utterances.* The performative sentences are:

    a. I testify that she met the agent.

    e. I dismiss the class.

    g. We promise to leave early.

    i. I bequeath $1,000,000 to the IRS.

    k. I swear I didn't do it.

18. *Grice's Maxims.*

    A. This example is similar to the example "Can you pass the salt?" in the textbook. In this case, asking someone what cookie crumbs are doing, if answered literally, would force the responder into stating the obvious, which is exactly what the child in this dialogue does—in violation of the maxim of quantity, with humorous effect.

    B. In this example, the maxim of relevance is key. When the woman says, "If cats ruled the world, everyone would sleep on a pile of fresh laundry," she is presupposing that cats do not rule the world. This, however, surprises the cat, who then questions her presupposition. The presupposition was probably not surprising to the reader/listener, so the cat pointing it out is humorous.

19. *Grice's Maxims in the wild.*

    A. Answers will vary. Here are a few I found in my own home:

      a. Child: "Mama, will you play with me?" Mama: "Sorry, honey, but my hands are full." In order not to be violating the maxim of relevance, the mother is really saying, "I can't/won't play with you right now because my hands are full."

      b. Mama, yelling in the house: "Dinner is ready!" In order to not just be violating the maxim of quantity, in this case announcing the state of affairs for no apparent reason, the mother must mean, "Dinner is ready, so come to the table now and eat it."

      c. Wife to husband, "Did you remember it was garbage day today?" In order to not be violating the maxim of relevance, and forcing the husband to answer whether or not he remembered that the day was garbage day, the wife must really mean, "Did you take the garbage out today?"

    B. The shopkeeper seems to be unwilling (or unable) to interpret intended meanings of utterances that violate Grice's maxims. For example, Nick Charles' statement "goodbye now" violates the maxim of quantity, since the "now" part is obvious and redundant, but this violation probably would not bother most people. The shopkeeper, though, is quite bothered and points out this violation. Likewise, when Nick Charles calls the shopkeeper "brother," he is violating the maxim of quality, since this isn't technically true. Charles means it metaphorically, however, but the shopkeeper again can't or won't interpret it that way and

**56**

again points out the violation. Metaphor, in general, seems to upset the shopkeeper, who also appears to interpret "You got hold of somethin' there" only in its literal sense.

20. *Sentence interpretation.*
    **A.** a. red
       b. He shot him.
       c. He stabbed him.
       d. exhausted
    **B.** a. True
       b. False
       c. False
       d. False
       e. True
       f. False
       g. True

21. *Presuppositions.*
    a. We have been to the ball park before.
    b. Valerie did not receive a new T-bird for Labor Day.
    c. Emily had a pet turtle.
       Emily's pet turtle ran away.
    d. The administration once knew that the professors support the students.
       The professors support the students.
    e. The World Trade Center was attacked on September 11, 2001.
    f. The World Trade Center was attacked on September 11, 2001.
    g. Disa has had some popcorn already.
    h. Mary had at least one beer before that.
    i. Somebody discovered Pluto in 1930.
    j. Mary has a bed.
       Mary found a cockroach in her bed.

22. *Proforms.* Answers will vary. Here are some examples, but there are many others.
    **pro-verb:** *did*, because it can stand in for a verb, as in *John swam and Sally did, too.*
    **pro-adjective:** *like that* seems to function as a pro-adjective but must occur after the modified noun, as in:
       Person A: *I want a big, beautiful house.*
       Person B: *I want a house like that, too.*
    *Such* works similarly, but must come before the determiner, as in:
       Person A: *I want a big, beautiful house.*
       Person B: *I want such a house, too.*

57

**pro-adverb:** *so* can function as a pro-adverb, as in *John usually sings beautifully, and so he sang last Sunday. That way* is also a pro-adverb, as in *My mother wants me to frost the cake perfectly, but I'm not sure I can do it that way.*

23. *Talking in code.* When Alex tells Bruce "The eagle has landed," he is violating the maxims of relevance and manner. Bruce, then, has to choose whether to interpret Alex's comment literally as a completely irrelevant comment or realize that Alex is violating the maxim of relevance (by talking about eagles) and manner (but not saying directly and clearly what he means) intentionally, in order to be secretive. This type of talking in code works best when all parties involved have previously agreed upon the meanings of certain encoded phrases. Otherwise, even if the receiving party, like Bruce in our example, recognizes the utterance as encoded, he won't be able to decode it!

24. *Implicatures.*

   a. Statement: You make a better door than a window.
      Situation: Someone is blocking your view.
      Implicature: I want you to move out of the way.

   b. Statement: It's getting late.
      Situation: You're at a party and it's 4 A.M.
      Implicature: I'm ready to leave; let's leave (if said to one's friend(s)).

   c. Statement: The restaurants are open until midnight.
      Situation: It's 10 o'clock and you haven't eaten dinner.
      Implicature: Let's go eat at a restaurant.

   d. Statement: If you'd diet, this wouldn't hurt so badly.
      Situation: Someone is standing on your toe.
      Implicature: I want you to get off my toe.

   e. Statement: I thought I saw a fan in the closet.
      Situation: It's sweltering in the room.
      Implicature: Perhaps the fan could be put to use to make the room more comfortable.

   f. Statement: Mr. Smith dresses neatly, is well-groomed, and is always on time to class.
      Situation: The summary statement in a letter of recommendation to graduate school.
      Implicature: Mr. Smith cannot be recommended highly for his academic abilities.

   g. Statement: Most of the food is gone.
      Situation: You arrived late at a cocktail party.
      Implicature: I wish I had arrived earlier; I'd like something more to eat than what's left.

h. Statement: John or Mary made a mistake.
Situation: You're looking over some work done by John and Mary.
Implicature: One of the two, not the two together, is responsible for the mistake.

25. *Conversational implicatures.*

   a. Jack: Did you make a doctor's appointment?
   Laura: Their line was busy.
   Implicature: No.

   b. Jack: Do you have the play tickets?
   Laura: Didn't I give them to you?
   Implicature: I (Laura) don't have the tickets.

   c. Jack: Does your grandmother have a live-in boyfriend?
   Laura: She's very traditional.
   Implicature: No.

   d. Jack: How did you like the string quartet?
   Laura: I thought the violist was swell.
   Implicature: The quartet as whole wasn't very good.

   e. Laura: What are Boston's chances of winning the World Series?
   Jack: Do bowling balls float?
   Implicature: Boston has no chance.

   f. Laura: Do you own a cat?
   Jack: I'm allergic to everything.
   Implicature: No.

   g. Laura: Did you mow the grass and wash the car like I told you to?
   Jack: I mowed the grass.
   Implicature: I (Jack) didn't wash the car.

   h. Laura: Do you want dessert?
   Jack: Is the Pope Catholic?
   Implicature: Absolutely yes.

26.

   **A.** Think of ten negative polarity items such as *give a hoot* and *have a red cent*. Here are some examples.
   1. Jack hasn't been here *in years*. / *Jack has been here *in years*.
   2. Anna isn't back *yet*. / *Anna is back *yet*.
   3. She won't return *until* noon. / *She'll return *until* noon. (The *until* that appears in *She works until 5 P.M.* has a different meaning.)
   4. I don't like apricots *at all / anymore / much*. / *I like apricots *at all / anymore / much*. (Note that some dialects have a non-NPI use of *anymore* meaning 'now-a-days,' as in Philadelphian "Shoes are expensive anymore.")

5. Anna didn't *drink a drop / do a thing / lift a finger / bat an eye*. / *Anna *drank a drop / did a thing / lifted a finger / batted an eye*. (Note that these are okay with a literal meaning, but they can't have the idiomatic sense that they have in the negated sentences.)
6. I *would* not *mind* having a beer. / *I *would mind* having a beer.
7. I *need / dare* not have a beer. / *I *need / dare* have a beer.

B. **Challenge exercise.** Answers will vary. The major contexts are listed below, but there are many others. The negative polarity item in each example has been underlined.

1. Yes/no questions, and embedded yes/no questions

   Have you ever met <u>anyone</u> from Mali?
   John asked / wonders / knows whether Bill has ever met <u>anyone</u> from Mali.

2. Adverbial clauses (often with a "hypothetical" meaning)
   If <u>anyone</u> in this room has <u>ever</u> been to Paris . . .
   Whenever <u>anyone</u> in the room goes to Paris . . .
   Had <u>anyone</u> in this room <u>ever</u> been to Paris . . .
   Unless <u>anyone</u> in this room has <u>ever</u> been to Paris . . .

3. Comparatives, superlatives
   John is taller than <u>anyone</u> I've <u>ever</u> known.
   John is as tall as <u>anyone</u> I've <u>ever</u> known.
   John is the tallest man that I've <u>ever</u> known.

4. Universal determiners
   Every student who has <u>ever</u> been to Paris . . .
   Every student who has <u>any</u> friends . . .

27. **Challenge exercise.** Under this modified theory, Semantic Rule I determines that if the sentence *no baby sleeps* is true, then whatever thing the NP *no baby* refers to, call it Ø, must be a member of the meaning of the VP *sleeps*, i.e., a member of the set of individuals who sleep. Similarly for the sentence *no baby sleeps soundly*; if it is true, the thing referred to by *no baby* must be a member of the meaning of the VP *sleeps soundly*, i.e., a member of the set of individuals who sleep soundly. The set of individuals who sleep soundly are all individuals who sleep, so if the thing referred to by *no baby* is in the former set, it is in the latter. That is, if *no baby sleeps soundly* is true, then *no baby sleeps* is also true, under the modified theory. But in fact precisely the opposite is the case! *No baby sleeps* should entail that *no baby sleeps soundly* (and not vice versa). One of the goals of the semantic theory is to capture the entailment relations that speakers can recognize to hold between sentences, and it fails to achieve this goal if an NP like *no baby* is treated as referential in the same way that *the baby* is. It can be shown that analogous problems arise with treating any *quantified* NP (*some baby, every baby*, etc.) as referential.

28. *The meaning of words.* Students may respond freely. A possible answer might refer to Grice's Maxims and point out that sometimes we mean something different from what we are literally saying. For example, if we ask, "Can you pass me the salt?" there is nothing in the words per se that is asking the person to pass the salt. All that it is literally being asked is whether the person is able to pass the salt. We take the question to mean, "Will you pass me the salt?" not from the words themselves, but rather from our attitudes towards them, as de Saint-Exupery states.

29. *The Second Amendment of the Constitution.* Answers may vary.

    If the student disagrees, then it can be pointed out that the maxim of quantity means that in the minds of the writers of the amendment, the initial phrases *A well regulated Militia, being necessary to the security of a free State* are pertinent to the meaning of the entire amendment and place conditions of situation on the remaining *the right of the People to keep and bear Arms, shall not be infringed*, which is therefore not an absolute right. An extreme view might note that since there are no longer militias in the United States, the entire amendment is null and void and people have no right to bear arms whatsoever insofar as the Constitution is concerned.

    If the student agrees (in agreement with the U.S. courts), then the student may argue that the current method of defending the country with a full-time military no longer relies on militias, and that the maxim of relevance, together with that situation, dictates that the initial phrases be ignored, and that the final part of the amendment is without conditions, that is, absolute.

30. *Long-distance reflexives.* Apparent exceptions to the rule for reflexive pronouns presented in the chapter are not limited to the examples presented here. Many languages have cases where the antecedent of a reflexive pronoun and the reflexive pronoun itself have an intervening NP. Reflexives that participate in such constructions are called "long-distance reflexives." As long-distance reflexives occur in typologically diverse languages, linguists recognize that they should not be written off as an exception in one (or a few) languages, but rather that the theory of how pronouns and reflexives work in human language should account for these possibilities. Although such a theory is still in its infancy, what seems to be true of long-distance reflexives cross-linguistically is that they require their antecedent to be a subject and that they may occur in a restricted set of clause types (e.g., infinitival) in comparison with the regular reflexives. In many languages, long-distance reflexives are mono-morphemic, but as the English examples here show, this is not true of all long-distance reflexives.

# Chapter 5

1. *Initial sound.*

    a. judge [ʤ]
    b. Thomas [tʰ]
    c. though [ð]
    d. easy [i]
    e. pneumonia [n]

    f. thought [θ]
    g. contact [kʰ]
    h. phone [f]
    i. civic [s]
    j. usual [j]

2. *Final sound.*

    a. fleece [s]
    b. neigh [e] ~ [eɪ]
    c. long [ŋ]
    d. health [θ]
    e. watch [ʧ]

    f. cow [aʊ]
    g. rough [f]
    h. cheese [z]
    i. bleached [t]
    j. rags [z]

3. *Phonetic transcription.* Note: transcriptions may vary across dialects. For example, the *merry / marry / Mary* distinction is neutralized in many dialects in the United States.

    a. physics        [fɪzɪks]
    b. merry          [mɛri]
    c. marry          [mæri] ~ [mɛri]
    d. Mary           [meri] ~ [mɛri]
    e. yellow         [jɛlo]
    f. sticky         [stɪki]
    g. transcription  [trænskrɪpʃən]
    h. Fromkin        [frãmkɪn] ~ [frãmpkɪn]
    i. tease          [tʰiz]
    j. weather        [wɛðər]
    k. coat           [kʰot]
    l. Rodman         [radmə̃n]
    m. heath          [hiθ]
    n. (student's name)
    o. touch          [tʰʌʧ]
    p. cough          [kʰaf] ~ [kʰɔf]
    q. larynx         [lerĩŋks]
    r. through        [θru]
    s. beautiful      [bjutɪfəl]

t. honest [anɪst]
u. president [prɛzɪdẽnt] ~
[prɛzɪdĩnt] ~
[prɛzɪdõnt] ~
[prɛzədẽnt] ~
[prɛzədĩnt] ~
[prɛzədõnt]

4. *Correcting major errors in transcription.*

| Error | Correction |
|---|---|
| a. [cʌ̃m] | [kʰʌ̃m] |
| b. [sed] | [sɛd] |
| c. [tʰɔlk] | [tʰɔk] ~ [tʰak] |
| d. [ãnd] | [æ̃nd] |
| e. [wæx] | [wæks] |
| f. [kʰæbəgəz] | [kʰæbɚʤəz] |
| g. [ɪs] | [ɪz] |
| h. [wɛθər] | [wɛðər] |

5. *English orthography.*

a. [hit]  heat
b. [strok]  stroke
c. [fez]  phase ~ faze
d. [ton]  tone
e. [boni]  bony
f. [skrim]  scream
g. [frut]  fruit
h. [pritʃər]  preacher
i. [krak]  crock
j. [baks]  box
k. [θæŋks]  thanks
l. [wɛnzde]  Wednesday
m. [krɔld]  crawled
n. [kantʃiɛntʃəs]  conscientious
o. [parləmɛntæriən]  parliamentarian
p. [kwəbɛk]  Quebec
q. [pitsə]  pizza
r. [bərak obamə]  Barack Obama
s. [mɪt ramni]  Mitt Romney
t. [tu θauzənd ænd twɛlv]  two thousand and twelve

6. *Symbols for phonetic descriptions.*

| Description | Sound | Sample word |
|---|---|---|
| a. voiceless bilabial unaspirated stop | [p] | *spill* |
| b. low front vowel | [æ] | *tack* |

**63**

| | | | |
|---|---|---|---|
| c. | lateral liquid | [l] | *lip* |
| d. | velar nasal | [ŋ] | *sing* |
| e. | voiced interdental fricative | [ð] | *this* |
| f. | voiceless affricate | [ʧ] | *cherry* |
| g. | palatal glide | [j] | *yodel* |
| h. | mid lax front vowel | [ɛ] | *head* |
| i. | high back tense vowel | [u] | *food* |
| j. | voiceless aspirated alveolar stop | [tʰ] | *team* |

7. *Phonetic properties.*

   a. ba*th*—ba*th*e: The *th* in *bath* is voiceless; the *th* in *bathe* is voiced. Both are interdental fricatives.

   b. redu*c*e—redu*c*tion: The *c* in *reduce* is an alveolar fricative; the *c* in *reduction* is a velar stop. Both are voiceless obstruents.

   c. c*oo*l—c*o*ld: The *oo* in *cool* is high; the *o* in *cold* is mid. Both are tense, back, and rounded.

   d. wi*f*e—wi*v*es: The *f* in *wife* is voiceless; the *v* in *wives* is voiced. Both are labiodental fricatives.

   e. cat*s*—dog*s*: The *s* in *cats* is voiceless; the *s* in *dogs* is voiced. Both are alveolar fricatives (sibilants).

   f. i*m*polite—i*n*decent: The *m* in *impolite* is bilabial; the *n* in *indecent* is alveolar. Both are nasals.

8. *Transcriptions.*

| Written word | Transcription |
|---|---|
| know | [no] |
| tough | [tʰʌf] |
| bough | [baʊ] |
| cough | [kʰaf] ~ [kʰɔf] |
| dough | [do] |
| you | [ju] |
| hiccough | [hɪkəp] |
| thorough | [θʌro] |
| slough | [slu] ~ [slaʊ] ~ [slʌf] |
| through | [θru] |
| heard | [hərd] |
| word | [wərd] |
| beard | [bird] |
| bird | [bərd] |
| dead | [dɛd] |
| said | [sɛd] |
| bed | [bɛd] |

| | |
|---|---|
| bead | [bid] |
| deed | [did] |
| meat | [mit] |
| great | [gret] |
| threat | [θrɛt] |
| suite | [swit] |
| straight | [stret] |
| debt | [dɛt] |
| moth | [mɔθ] ~ [maθ] |
| mother | [mʌðər] |
| both | [boθ] |
| bother | [baðər] |
| broth | [brɔθ] ~ [braθ] |
| brother | [brʌðər] |

9. *Shared features.*

   a. [g] [p] [t] [d] [k] [b]  oral, stop, consonant

   b. [u] [ʊ] [o] [ɔ]  back, round, non-low, vowel

   c. [i] [ɪ] [e] [ɛ] [æ]  front, unrounded, vowel

   d. [t] [s] [ʃ] [p] [k] [tʃ] [f] [h]  voiceless, oral, obstruent, consonant

   e. [v] [z] [ʒ] [ʤ] [n] [g] [d] [b] [l] [r] [w] [j]  voiced, consonant

   f. [t] [d] [s] [ʃ] [n] [tʃ] [ʤ]  coronal, consonant

10. *Translating phonetics to spelling.*

    a. Noam Chomsky is a linguist who teaches at MIT.

    b. Phonetics is the study of speech sounds.

    c. All spoken languages use sounds produced by the upper respiratory system.

    d. In one dialect of English, *cot* the noun and *caught* the verb are pronounced the same.

    e. Some people think phonetics is very interesting.

    f. Victoria Fromkin, Robert Rodman, and Nina Hyams are the authors of this book.

11. *Phonetic features distinguishing sounds.*

| A | B |
|---|---|
| a. front | back |
| b. voiceless | voiced |
| c. labial | other places of articulation |
| d. high | nonhigh (mid and low) |
| e. continuant | noncontinuant |
| f. nonback (front and central) | back |

**65**

12. The pairs that have the same manner of articulation are: c (nasal); d (fricative); f (fricative); i (glide).

13. *Tense and lax vowels.*

### Part One

| | | |
|---|---|---|
| a. | [i] | tense |
| b. | [ɪ] | lax |
| c. | [u] | tense |
| d. | [ʌ] | lax |
| e. | [ʊ] | lax |
| f. | [e] | tense |
| g. | [ɛ] | lax |
| h. | [o] | tense |
| i. | [ɔ] | lax |
| j. | [æ] | lax |
| k. | [a] | tense |
| l. | [ə] | lax |
| m. | [aɪ] | tense |
| n. | [aʊ] | tense |
| o. | [ɔɪ] | tense |

### Part Two. Answers will vary.

| | Vowel | Sample word |
|---|---|---|
| a. | [i] | *leash* [liʃ] |
| b. | [ɪ] | *fish* [fɪʃ] |
| c. | [u] | *Koosh* [kuʃ] (as in Koosh ball, the popular novelty ball from the 80s) and *smoosh* [smuʃ] (a slang variant for *smush* [smʊʃ]); potentially does not exist in English outside of these two examples |
| d. | [ʌ] | *mush* [mʌʃ] |
| e. | [ʊ] | *push* [pʊʃ] |
| f. | [e] | potentially does not exist in English |
| g. | [ɛ] | *mesh* [mɛʃ] |
| h. | [o] | potentially does not exist in English, but note *gauche* [goʃ] (borrowed, but in common use) |
| i. | [ɔ] | *wash* [wɔʃ], in some dialects |
| j. | [æ] | *ash* [æʃ] |
| k. | [a] | *posh* [paʃ] |
| l. | [ə] | potentially does not exist in English |
| m. | [aɪ] | potentially does not exist in English |
| n. | [aʊ] | potentially does not exist in English |
| o. | [ɔɪ] | potentially does not exist in English |

**Part Three.** The majority of such words have lax vowels.

14. *Sentence with monophthongs and diphthongs. Answers will vary.* Sample answer: "The old brown dog chased my big cat." [ðə old braʊn dag ʧʰest maɪ bɪg kʰæt]

15. *Transcribing French.*

| French word | Transcription |
|---|---|
| *tu* 'you' | [ty] |
| *bleu* 'blue' | [blø] |
| *heure* 'hour' | [œʀ] or [œr] |

16. **Challenge exercise.** *Monosyllabic words containing vowels followed by [t], [r], and [ŋ].*

A. *Monosyllabic words containing vowels followed by [t].* (Some speakers may not have a word such as [bɔt], *bought,* always using the vowel [a] or even a vowel intermediate between [ɔ] and [a] where other speakers have both vowels.) Answers will vary.

| Vowel | Sample word |
|---|---|
| i | *meet* [mit] |
| ɪ | *bit* [bɪt] |
| e | *mate* [met] |
| ɛ | *met* [mɛt] |
| æ | *mat* [mæt] |
| u | *moot* [mut] |
| ʊ | *foot* [fʊt] |
| ʌ | *hut* [hʌt] |
| o | *moat* [mot] |
| ɔ | *bought* [bɔt] |
| a | *pot* [pat] |
| aɪ | *fight* [faɪt] |
| aʊ | *grout* [graʊt] |
| ɔɪ | *Hoyt* [hɔɪt], a man's name. Also a dialectal pronunciation of *hurt.* |

B. *Monosyllabic words containing vowels followed by [r].* (There is much dialectal variation in these choices. The answers given reflect one dialect of American English of several possibilities. What is generally observed is that speakers will choose one phoneme from a given tense-lax pair, but the other will not occur. So if the speaker uses [i], she will not also use [ɪ]; or if she uses [ɛ] she will not also use [e], and so on for [u] and [ʊ], and [a] and [ʌ]. However, the choice of tense versus lax is not consistent, as this particular dialect shows.) Answers will vary.

| Vowel | Sample word |
|---|---|
| i | *ear* [ir] |
| ɪ | does not occur in this dialect |

| | |
|---|---|
| e | does not occur in this dialect |
| ɛ | *hair* [hɛr] |
| æ | does not occur in this dialect |
| u | does not occur in this dialect |
| ʊ | *sure* [ʃʊr] |
| ʌ | does not occur in this dialect |
| o | does not occur in this dialect |
| ɔ | *bore* [bɔr] |
| a | *bar* [bar] |
| aɪ | *hire* [haɪr], but some speakers may pronounce this word with two syllables |
| aʊ | *our* [aʊr], but some speakers may pronounce this word with two syllables |
| ɔɪ | *foyer* [fɔɪr], but some speakers may pronounce this word with two syllables |

C. *Monosyllabic words containing vowels followed by [ŋ].* Similar comments regarding dialectal variation and tense/lax choices apply here as noted in part B. Answers will vary.

| Vowel | Sample word |
|---|---|
| i | does not occur in this dialect |
| ɪ | *sing* [sɪŋ] |
| e | does not occur in this dialect |
| ɛ | *length* [lɛŋθ] |
| æ | *sang* [sæŋ] |
| u | does not occur in this dialect |
| ʊ | does not occur in this dialect |
| ʌ | *rung* [rʌŋ] |
| o | does not occur in this dialect |
| ɔ | *wrong* [rɔŋ] |
| a | does not occur in this dialect |
| aɪ | does not occur in this dialect |
| aʊ | does not occur in this dialect |
| ɔɪ | does not occur in this dialect |

D. *Quantitative differences.* Yes. There is a greater variety of vowels preceding [t] than preceding [r]. Likewise, there are more vowels preceding [r] than [ŋ].

E. In B all but three vowels [ɛ, ʊ, ɔ] are tense; in C all the vowels are lax.

F. *Summary of difficulties.* Answers will vary. Sample answer:

It was much easier to find words with [Vt] then it was to find words with [Vr] or [Vŋ]. It was much harder to hear the tense/lax vowel distinction before [r] and [ŋ], which made it difficult to find words. Also, there is dialectal variation, so an attempt to query other persons may lead to conflicting results.

17. *Matching names and works.*

      a—1      (Dickens, *Oliver Twist*)
      b—4      (Cervantes, *Don Quixote)*
      c—11    (Dante, *The Divine Comedy*)
      d—6      (Dickens, *Great Expectations*)
      e—10    (Eliot, *Silas Marner*)
      f—2      (Hemingway, *A Farewell to Arms*)
      g—12    (Homer, *The Iliad*)
      h—9      (Melville, *Moby Dick*)
      i—3      (Orwell, *Animal Farm*)
      j—8      (Shakespeare, *Hamlet*)
      k—5      (Steinbeck, *Grapes of Wrath*)
      l—7      (Swift, *Gulliver's Travels*)
      m—14    (Tolstoy, *War and Peace*)
      n—13    (Twain, *Tom Sawyer*)

# Chapter 6

1. *Minimal pairs.* Sample answers:

| | Initial | Medial | Final |
|---|---|---|---|
| a. /k/—/g/ | cold/gold | bicker/bigger | tuck/tug |
| b. /m/—/n/ | mice/nice | simmer/sinner | sum/sun |
| c. /l/—/r/ | lake/rake | cold/cord | feel/fear |
| d. /b/—/v/ | ban/van | saber/saver | dub/dove |
| e. /b/—/m/ | ban/man | clabber/clamor | rub/rum |
| f. /p/—/f/ | pail/fail | supper/suffer | leap/leaf |
| g. /s/—/ʃ/ | sell/shell | masses/mashes | lease/leash |
| h. /tʃ/—/dʒ/ | chin/gin | etches/edges | rich/ridge |
| i. /s/—/z/ | sip/zip | fussy/fuzzy | mace/maze |

2. *Rules relating spelling to pronunciation.* In the patient's system of spelling-to-pronunciation, the following are true:

**In reading:**
- *a* corresponds to /a/ or /æ/
- medial *e* corresponds to /ɛ/
- final *e* corresponds to /i/
- *i* corresponds to /aɪ/
- *o* corresponds to /o/ or /ɔ/
- *c* corresponds to /s/
- every letter is pronounced
- there is one vowel per syllable

**In writing from dictation:**
- /e/ and /æ/ correspond to written A
- /aɪ/ corresponds to written I
- /i/ corresponds to written E
- /o/ corresponds to written O
- /k/ corresponds to written K
- no silent letters are written, e.g., final *e*
- /z/ is written as Z even when spelled *s* in an inflectional morpheme

**70**

3. *Complementary Distribution and "A Case of Identity."* Sherlock Homes solved the mystery of Miss Mary Sutherland's missing fiancé by noting that Mr. Hosmer Angel (the missing fiancé) and Mr. James Windibank were in complementary distribution, i.e. they never appeared in the same place at the same time. As Sherlock Holmes points out, "[T]he fact that the two men were never together, but that the one always appeared when the other was away, was suggestive." The complementary distribution of these two "individuals" together with the fact that they shared certain physical traits and they both used a typewriter with the same characteristics led Sherlock Holmes to conclude that Mr. Hosmer Angel and Mr. James Windibank are in fact the same person.

So just as two sounds, sharing some features in common, that are in complementary distribution do not contrast and are not distinct phonemes, Mr. Angel and Mr. Windibank are not distinct people.

4. *Korean.*

   **Part One**

   a. [r] and [l] are allophones of one phoneme.

   b. No, they do not occur in any minimal pairs.

   c. Yes, [r] and [l] are in complementary distribution.

   d. [r] occurs before vowels. [l] occurs before consonants and word finally.

   e. The phoneme /l/ is realized phonetically as [r] when it occurs before a vowel, and as [l] in all other instances. This rule can be written as follows:

   $$/l/ \rightarrow [r] / \underline{\quad} V$$

   Note it is not necessary to include a rule that specifies where the allophone [l] occurs since /l/ will not be changed pre-consonantally or finally and will emerge phonetically as [l]. Note further that if the two allophones are derived from /r/, the rule would be more complex:

   $$/r/ \rightarrow [l] / \underline{\quad} \left\{ \begin{matrix} C \\ \# \end{matrix} \right\}$$

   **Part Two**

   a. [s] and [ʃ] are allophones of the same phoneme. They are in complementary distribution: [ʃ] appears before [i] and [s] appears before all other vowels or word finally.

   b. This distribution can be written as the following phonemic rule:

   $$/s/ \rightarrow [ʃ] / \underline{\quad} [i]$$

5. *German [x] and [ç].*

   a. [x] and [ç] are allophones of the same phoneme. They are in complementary distribution. [x] only occurs after non-front vowels and [ç] only occurs after front vowels.

b. The most natural rule to account for the data is:

$$/x/ \rightarrow [\varsigma] \Bigg/ \begin{bmatrix} V \\ -back \\ -central \end{bmatrix} \underline{\quad}$$

6. *English plural morphemes.*

If Rule B is reformulated as below (and Rule A remains the same, as shown below), then the ordering between these rules won't matter. However, the reformulation is less simple and less elegant. The plural morpheme /z/ becomes an [s], assimilating to the voicelessness of the preceding consonant. The revision of the rule suggests that only voiceless non-sibilants trigger this assimilation, which doesn't seem entirely correct.

A. Insert a [ə] before the plural morpheme /z/ when a regular noun ends in a sibilant, giving [əz].

B. Change the plural morpheme /z/ to a voiceless [s] when preceded by a voiceless, non-sibilant sound.

7. *Southern Kongo.*

a. Distributions:

[t]—[tʃ]:    [t] occurs before [o], [a], [e], and [u]; [tʃ] occurs before [i].

[s]—[ʃ]:    [s] occurs before [o], [u], and [e]; [ʃ] occurs before [i].

[z]—[ʒ]:    [z] occurs before [u], [e], and [w]; [ʒ] occurs before [i].

b. In each pair, the nonpalatal segment should be used as the basic phoneme (e.g., [t] and [tʃ] derived from /t/, [s] and [ʃ] derived from /s/, and [z] and [ʒ] derived from /z/). Nonpalatal segments have a wider (less specific) distribution, so the phonemic rule will be simpler with the nonpalatal segment as the "elsewhere" (default) case.

c. One phonemic rule that will account for all of the above distributions is the following:

**Obstruent alveolar segments become palatalized before a high front vowel.**

This can be stated formally as:

$$\begin{bmatrix} +alveolar \\ -sonorant \end{bmatrix} \rightarrow \begin{bmatrix} -alveolar \\ +palatal \end{bmatrix} \Bigg/ \underline{\quad} \begin{bmatrix} +high \\ -back \end{bmatrix}$$

d. i. not a possible word, because [s] does not occur before [i] in Southern Kongo

ii. not a possible word, because [tʃ] does not occur before [u]

iii. is a possible word

iv. is a possible word

v. is a possible word

vi. is not a possible word, because [ʒ] does not occur before [a]

**72**

8. *English [aɪ] ~ [ʌɪ].*

   a. The final sounds in column A are [−voice] and those in column B are [+voice].

   b. The words in column C end in vowels.

   c. Yes. [ʌɪ] and [aɪ] are in complementary distribution: their distribution is predictable. [ʌɪ] occurs before voiceless segments, and [aɪ] occurs elsewhere, i.e., before voiced segments or word finally.

   d. They should be derived from /aɪ/. [aɪ] has a wider distribution than [ʌɪ]. Also, it is easier to characterize the distribution of [ʌɪ] than the distribution of [aɪ], so the phonemic rule will be simpler if [aɪ] is the sound occurring "elsewhere."

   e. life [lʌɪf]      lives [laɪvz]      lie [laɪ]
      file [faɪl]      bike [bʌɪk]      lice [lʌɪs]

   f. /aɪ/ → [ʌɪ] / ___ [−voice]

9. *English palatalization.* Palatalization occurs whenever /t/, /d/, /s/, and /z/ (alveolar obstruents) are followed by the palatal glide /j/.

$$\begin{bmatrix} +alveolar \\ -sonorant \end{bmatrix} \rightarrow \begin{bmatrix} -alveolar \\ +palatal \end{bmatrix} / \underline{\quad} \begin{bmatrix} +sonorant \\ -palatal \end{bmatrix}$$

10. *Japanese [t] ~ [tʃ] ~ [ts].*

    a. Yes, these sounds, [t], [tʃ], and [ts] are in complementary distribution as they never occur in the same environments.

    b. [tʃ] occurs before [i], [ts] occurs before [u], and [t] occurs elsewhere (before vowels that are non-high). In features, [tʃ] occurs before [−consonantal, +high, −back] segments, [ts] occurs before [−consonantal, +high, +back] segments, and [t] occurs before [−consonantal, −high] segments.

    c. [t], [tʃ], and [ts] are allophones of a single phoneme, which we will represent with /t/ since the [t] allophone has the widest distribution of the three. The allophones are derived according to the rules below:

    1) /t/ → [tʃ] / ___ $\begin{bmatrix} +high \\ -back \end{bmatrix}$

    2) /t/ → [ts] / ___ $\begin{bmatrix} +high \\ -back \end{bmatrix}$

    d.
    | | | | | | |
    |---|---|---|---|---|---|
    | tatami | /tatami/ | tsukue | /tukue/ | tsutsumu | /tutumu/ |
    | tomodatʃi | /tomodati/ | tetsudau | /tetudau/ | tʃizu | /tizu/ |
    | utʃi | /uti/ | ʃita | /ʃita/ | kata | /kata/ |
    | tegami | /tegami/ | ato | /ato/ | koto | /koto/ |
    | totemo | /totemo/ | matsu | /matu/ | tatemono | /tatemono/ |
    | otoko | /otoko/ | degutʃi | /deguti/ | te | /te/ |
    | tʃitʃi | /titi/ | natsu | /natu/ | tsuri | /turi/ |

73

11. *Paku.*

    i. Yes, stress is predictable. It falls on the penultimate (next to last) syllable.

    ii. No, nasalization is not a distinctive feature for vowels as it is predictable. A vowel is nasalized if it precedes a nasal consonant.

    iii. Plurals are formed by adding the suffix *-ni*. Note that the addition of this suffix can affect the nasalization of the preceding vowel, given the rule in (ii), and will change where stress falls in a word, given the rule in (i).

12. *English stress.*

    a. The following are essentially phonemic transcriptions, except for [ə], the symbol for all unstressed vowels.

| A | B | C |
|---|---|---|
| /əstanɪʃ/ | /kəlæps/ | /əmez/ |
| /ɛgzət/ | /ɛgzɪst/ | /ɪmpruv/ |
| /ɪmæʤən/ | /rəzent/ | /sərpraɪz/ |
| /kænsəl/ | /rəvolt/ | /kəmbaɪn/ |
| /əlɪsət/ | /ədapt/ | /bəliv/ |
| /præktəs/ | /ɪnsɪst/ | /əton/ |

    b. The final syllable of the verb is stressed if it ends with a consonant cluster; otherwise, the stress falls on the penultimate syllable.

    c. All of the final vowels in column C are tense vowels. Thus, the analysis in (b) must be modified to read: Stress the final syllable of a verb if its vowel is tense or followed by a consonant cluster; otherwise stress the penultimate syllable.

13. *English phonotactics.*

| | | Word | Possible | Not Possible | Reason |
|---|---|---|---|---|---|
| a. | [pʰril] | | | x | |
| b. | [skritʃ] | screech | | | |
| c. | [kʰno] | | | x | English phonotactic rules prohibit an initial cluster composed of two stops. |
| d. | [maɪ] | my | | | |
| e. | [gnostɪk] | | | x | English phonotactic rules prohibit an initial cluster composed of two stops. |
| f. | [jũnəkʰɔrn] | unicorn | | | |
| g. | [fruit] | | | x | A glide always occurs between front and back high vowels in English. |
| h. | [blaft] | | x | | |
| i. | [ŋar] | | | x | English phonotactic rules do not permit the velar nasal to occur word-initially. |
| j. | [æpəpʰlɛksi] | apoplexy | | | |

**74**

14. *Hebrew.*

   a. [b] and [v] are allophones of one phoneme and are in complementary distribution.

   [b] occurs word-initially and after consonants while [v] occurs only after vowels.

   $$/b/ \rightarrow [v] / V \_\_$$

   b. Yes, [f] occurs only after vowels, [p] occurs word-initially and after consonants.

   c. The correct statement is (i): [b] but not [v] could occur in the empty slot.

   d. The correct statement is (ii): [p] but not [f] could occur in the empty slot.

   e. The correct statement is (i). These words would force you to revise conclusions reached on the basis of the first group of words since they show a distribution of sounds that differ from the first group: [b] occurring after a vowel, [v] occurring after a consonant, and [f] occurring word-initially. If we were doing a full analysis, we would therefore have to examine additional data not supplied here to formulate the correct analysis.

15. *Maninka.*

   a. (1) -*li*

   (2) -*ni*

   b. Yes, the phonetic variants are predictable. The form is -*ni* if the last consonant of the stem is a nasal and -*li* otherwise. Notice that the last consonant of the stem does not have to be the last segment of the stem for the nasalized variant to appear.

   c. da 'lie down'      dali 'lying down'
      men 'hear'         menni 'hearing'
      famu 'understand'  famuni 'understanding'
      sunogo 'sleep'     sunogoli 'sleeping'

   d. The rule formulated above in (b) above predicts the form *sunogoli* 'sleeping' because the last consonant of the stem is not a nasal.

   e. In order to predict the form *sunogoni* 'sleeping' without affecting the other cases, the rule can be reformulated as follows: The form is -*ni* if there is a nasal consonant somewhere in the stem and -*li* otherwise. If you happened to give the former as your rule, thus predicting *sunogoni*, then change it to the rule in (b) to derive *sunogoli*.

16. *Luganda.*

   a. No, nasal vowels are not phonemic in Luganda. Yes, they are predictable since they only occur before nasal consonants.

   b. Yes, the phonemic representation of 'garden' is /dimiro/.

   c. The phonemic representation of 'canoe' is /ato/.

d. [p] and [b] represent separate phonemes and not allophones of one phoneme because their occurrence is not predictable and they are not in complementary distribution. Both sounds occur in phonetically similar environments.

e. No, [ãmdãno] is not a possible phonetic form because [d] cannot follow [m] since sequences of a nasal consonant followed by a voiced oral consonant do not occur, and the place of articulation does not agree.

f. Yes, there is a homorganic rule in Luganda.

g. Phonemic: /enpoːbe/ Phonetic: [empoːbe]

h. (i) /en/

i. [ẽntabi]

j. /akaugeni/

k. Rule 1: Vowel nasalization: a vowel is nasalized when it precedes a nasal consonant.

 Rule 2: Homorganic nasal rule: /n/ assimilates to the place of articulation of a following consonant.

 Rule 3: Voiced stop assimilation: A voiced stop becomes a nasal if preceded by a nasal consonant.

17. *Japanese morphophonemics.* (Cf. exercise 10.)

 a.

| 'call' | /yob/ |
| 'write' | /kak/ |
| 'eat' | /tabe/ |
| 'see' | /mi/ |
| 'leave' | /de/ |
| 'go out' | /dekake/ |
| 'die' | /sin/ |
| 'close' | /sime/ |
| 'swindle' | /kata/ |
| 'wear' | /ki/ |
| 'read' | /yom/ |
| 'lend' | /kas/ |
| 'wait' | /mat/ |
| 'press' | /os/ |
| 'apply' | /ate/ |
| 'drop' | /otos/ |
| 'have' | /mot/ |
| 'win' | /kat/ |
| 'steal a lover' | /neto/ |

 b. i. /t/ → [ts] / ___ [u]

 ii. /t/ → [tʃ] / ___ [i]

 iii. /s/ → [ʃ] / ___ [i]

c. i. Formal: The allomorphs are [imasu] and [masu]. The rule is:

$$/imasu/ \rightarrow [masu] / V \underline{\quad}$$

ii. Informal: The allomorphs are [ru] and [u]. The rule is:

$$/ru/ \rightarrow [u] / C \underline{\quad}$$

18. *Ojibwa.*

a. The morpheme 'I' has the allomorphs [nit] and [ni].
The morpheme 'you' has the allomorphs [kiʃ] and [ki].

b. Yes, the allomorphs for 'I' are in complementary distribution. Their distribution is predictable; [nit] occurs before vowels, and [ni] occurs before consonants. The allomorphs for 'you' are also in complementary distribution. Their distribution is predictable: [kiʃ] occurs before vowels, and [ki] occurs before consonants.

c. /nit/ and /kiʃ/ are the underlying morphemes.

d. Delete a consonant before another consonant, or more formally:

$$C \rightarrow \emptyset / \underline{\quad} C$$

e. Yes, most likely the rule is morphophonemic. If the rule applied in general, rather than to specific morphemes, the language wouldn't have long (doubled) consonants such as [kː] and [ʃː] since they could be regarded as a CC cluster and the rule would delete the first C.

19. *Myanmar nasals.*

There is a four-way contrast between the phones [m], [m̥], [n], and [n̥], clearly exemplified by the following minimal set:

[ma] 'health'
[m̥a] 'order'
[na] 'pain'
[n̥a] 'nostril'

This set shows that these four phones belong to four separate phonemes. There is a pair of words that at first pass might seem to contradict this conclusion:

[mi] ~ [m̥i] 'flame'

However, this data isn't a counterexample to our previous conclusion. The minimal set presented above proves that these four phones contrast. The various pronunciations of 'flame' just show that these phones don't always have to contrast. (We see similar examples in English. For example, we know that [ɛ] and [i] belong to separate phonemes in English, as shown by the minimal pair [bɛn] 'Ben' and [bin] 'bean'. However, the word *economics* can be pronounced either

77

[ɛkənamɪks] or [ikənamɪks]. Note that the alternation of [ɛ] and [i] here doesn't change the meaning of the word. Nevertheless [ɛ] and [i] contrast in English.)

20. *Wakanti.*

    a. The phonemic form of the negative morpheme is /n/.

    b. The allomorphs are [n], [m], [ŋ].

    c. The nasal consonant [n] assimilates in place of articulation to the following consonant. For example, /n/ will become [m] before a labial, [ŋ] before a velar, and remain [n] elsewhere. Note: /w/ is considered a labial consonant in this language.

    d. Oral voiced stops will become nasal after a nasal consonant. For example, /indeɪ/ will become [inneɪ].

    e.
| | |
|---|---|
| /anba/ | 'I don't eat' |
| /indeɪ/ | 'You don't sleep' |
| /anguʊ/ | 'I don't go' |
| /unpi/ | 'We don't come' |
| /antu/ | 'I don't walk' |
| /inka/ | 'You don't see' |
| /injama/ | 'You didn't find out' |
| /anweli/ | 'I didn't climb up' |
| /inoa/ | 'You didn't fall' |
| /anie/ | 'I don't hunt' |
| /unlamaba/ | 'We don't put on top' |

21. *French*

    a. The two forms for 'small' are [pəti] and [pətit]. The two forms for 'our' are [no] and [noz].

    b. [pəti] occurs before words that begin with: [t], [l], [n]
       [no] occurs before words that begin with: [t], [l], [n]
       [pətit] occurs before words that begin with: [w], [a]
       [noz] occurs before words that begin with: [w], [a]

    c. [pəti] and [no] occur when the following word begins with an obstruent, liquid, or nasal consonant. [pətit] and [noz] occur when the following word begins with a vowel or a glide. We can summarize this by saying that [pəti] and [no] occur:
       / ___ [+consonantal] (before a +consonantal segment)
       and [pətit] and [noz] occur:
       / ___ [−consonantal] (before a non-consonantal segment).

    d. The basic forms must be the forms that end in consonants— [pətit] 'small' and [noz] 'our'— because we can make a generalization that

**78**

deletes the word-final consonant in both cases, but we cannot make a generalization that inserts a [t] in one case and a [z] in the other.

e. Delete the final consonant of a word if it occurs before a word that starts with an obstruent, liquid, or nasal consonant.

f. C → ∅ / ___ ##[+consonantal]

22. *English /b/ deletion.*

a. The two allomorphs of each root morpheme are:
   [bãm] ~ [bãmb]
   [kʰrʌ̃m] ~ [kʰrʌ̃mb]
   [aɪæ̃m] ~ [aɪæ̃mb]
   [θʌ̃m] ~ [θʌ̃mb]
   [rãm] ~ [rãmb]
   [tũm] ~ [tũmb]

b. The phonemic form of the roots are:
   /bamb/
   /krʌmb/
   /aɪæmb/
   /θʌmb/
   /ramb/
   /tumb/

c. The /b/ is deleted when it occurs at the end of the word.

d. [bãm] 'bomb'            [bãmb + ard] 'bombard'
   [kʰrʌ̃m] 'crumb'         [kʰrʌ̃mb + əl] 'crumble'
   [aɪæ̃m] 'iamb'           [aɪæ̃mb + ɪc] 'iambic'
   [θʌ̃m] 'thumb'           [θʌ̃mb + əlĭnə] 'Thumbelina'
   [rãm] 'rhomb'           [rãmb + ɔɪd] 'rhomboid'
   [tũm] 'tomb'            [tũmb + əl] 'tombal'

23. *Hebrew metathesis.*

a. The phonological change taking place is metathesis.

b. This is an example of metathesis. When the reflexive *lehit* is added to the sibilant-initial verbs, the last sound of the reflexive metathesizes with the initial sound of the verb root.

24. *Japanese vowel devoicing.*

a. [u] and [i] may occur voiceless.

b. Yes, the voiceless vowels are in complementary distribution. The voiceless vowels occur between voiceless consonants as in [fu̥kuan] 'a plan.' The voiced vowels appear elsewhere, as in [fugi] 'discuss.'

c. Yes, [u] and [y̥], and [i] and [i̥], are allophones because they are in complimentary distribution, and are phonetically similar, differing in only one feature (voice).

d. High vowels (/u/ and /i/) become voiceless when they are between voiceless consonants. This rule can be stated formally as

$$\begin{bmatrix} V \\ +\text{high} \\ +\text{voiced} \end{bmatrix} \rightarrow [-\text{voice}] \Big/ \begin{bmatrix} C \\ +\text{voice} \end{bmatrix} - \begin{bmatrix} C \\ +\text{voice} \end{bmatrix}$$

25. *Plural and past tense rules of English.* Answers should include some mention of faithfulness constraints. A faithfulness constraint is acting to preserve the underlying plural /z/ and the underlying past tense /d/.

26. *Ranking of constraints in English versus German.* A faithfulness constraint—that underlying forms surface intact—outranks the constraint *Voiced obstruents are not permitted at the end of a word* in English, but not in German.

27. *The "[dɔgs]" dialect of English.* For speakers of English who permit words such as [dɔgs], the constraint *Voiced obstruents separated by a morpheme boundary are not permitted at the end of a word* is ranked higher than for those who only allow forms such as [dɔgz].

    In particular, it outranks the faithfulness constraint that would preserve the /z/, and the constraint *Obstruent sequences may not differ with respect to their voice feature at the end of a word.*

28. *German.* Both German and English obey the constraint: *Obstruent sequences may not differ with respect to their voice feature at the end of a word.* In English, it is the final segment of the *stem* that conditions the past tense morpheme to devoice (/sɪp+d/ → [sɪpt], *sipped*), while in German, the third-person *suffix* conditions devoicing of the final segment of the stem /loːb+t/ → [loːpt].

# Chapter 7

1. *Variation in English.* Answers will vary considerably, depending on the dialect of the student. Transcriptions are given in two sample dialects: Dialect A is the one represented in the original question and Dialect B is another American English dialect.

| | Word | Transcriptions | | Word | Transcriptions | |
|---|---|---|---|---|---|---|
| | | Dialect A | Dialect B | | Dialect A | Dialect B |
| a. | horse | [hɔrs] | [hors] | hoarse | [hors] | [hɔrs] |
| b. | morning | [mɔrnĩŋ] | [mornĩŋ] | mourning | [mɔrnĩŋ] | [mornĩŋ] |
| c. | for | [fɔr] | [for] | four | [for] | [fɔr] |
| d. | ice | [ʌɪs] | [aɪs] | eyes | [aɪz] | [aɪz] |
| e. | knife | [nʌɪf] | [naɪf] | knives | [naɪvz] | [naɪvz] |
| f. | mute | [mjut] | [mut] | nude | [njud] | [nud] |
| g. | din | [dĩn] | [dɛ̃n] | den | [dɛ̃n] | [dĩn] |
| h. | hog | [hɔg] | [hag] | hot | [hat] | [hɔt] |
| i. | marry | [mæri] | [mɛri] | Mary | [meri] | [mɛri] |
| j. | merry | [mɛri] | [mɛri] | marry | [mæri] | [mɛri] |
| k. | rot | [rat] | [rat] | wrought | [rɔt] | [rɔt] |
| l. | lease | [lis] | [lis] | grease (v.) | [griz] | [gris] |
| m. | what | [ʌat] | [wat] | watt | [wat] | [wat] |
| n. | ant | [ænt] | [ænt] | aunt | [ãnt] | [ænt] |
| o. | creek | [kʰrɪk] | [kʰrik] | creak | [kʰrik] | [kʰrik] |

2. A. *Cameroon English Pidgin and Standard American English.*

*Some Similarities*: Many of the words in the CEP passage are derived from English words, such as *tok* 'talk,' *gud* 'good,' *nuus* 'news.' The word order seems to be SVO, as in English: *mek yi rud tret* 'make his road straight.' CEP has prepositional phrases, as English does: *bifo you fes* 'before your face.'

*Some Differences*: Some of the words in CEP are taken from the language of Cameroon rather than English, for example, *nchinda*, which means 'prophet.' In CEP, the word *yi* indicates possession (*God yi nchinda*—'God's prophet'), while in SAE either *'s* or a PP with *of* is used. Many sounds of SAE do not exist in CEP: for example, SAE *th* ([ð]) is *d* in CEP (*di*—*the*), and the word-final *r* of SAE is deleted in CEP (*weh*—'where'). Also, the cluster *str* is simplified in CEP to *tr* in the word *tret* ('straight'). The SAE indefinite article *a* is replaced by *som* in CEP.

B. *Tok Pisin derivations.*

| Tok Pisin | Gloss | Answer |
|---|---|---|
| taim bilong kol | winter | time belong cold |
| pinga bilong fut | toe | finger belong foot |
| hamas krismas yu gat? | how old are you? | how much Christmas you got? |
| kukim long paia | barbeque | cook them long fire |
| sapos | if | suppose |
| haus moni | bank | house money |
| kamup | arrive | come up |
| tasol | only | that's all |
| olgeta | all | all together |
| solwara | sea | salt water |
| haus sik | hospital | house sick |
| handet yia | century | hundred year |

3. *American slang.* Answers will vary quite a bit depending on the students' dialect and age. Note that in the answers given below, part (1) answers whether or not the word or phrase still exists with an idiomatic meaning. For example, *pipe layer* no longer has an idiomatic meaning, so the answer to part (1) for that item is *no*, even though the word still has its literal sense.

- *all out* (completely): (1) Yes; (3) *All out* still means 'completely' but is more restricted in use; the phrase *all out the best* does not occur in modern speech. Phrases like *go all out* are common, but *all out* occurs only with a small set of verbs (*go, play, run*).
- *to have apartments to let* (be an idiot): (1) No; (2) *the lights are on but nobody's home; there's nothing upstairs; not playing with a full deck.*
- *been there* (experienced): (1) Yes.
- *belly-button* (navel): (1) Yes.
- *berkeleys* (a woman's breasts): (1) No; (2) *knockers, tits, boobs.*
- *bitch* (offensive name for a woman): (1) Yes; (3) but *whore* is more offensive than *bitch* now; *bitch* can even be used as a term of endearment, usually between close girlfriends.
- *once in a blue moon* (seldom): (1) Yes.
- *boss* (master): (1) Yes; (3) *boss* can also mean 'nice' as in *dude, the iPhone 5 is boss.*
- *bread* (employment): (1) Yes; (3) *Bread* as a slang term now refers to money rather than employment.
- *claim* (steal): (1) No; (2) *rip off, cop, lift, jack.*
- *cut dirt* (escape): (1) No; (2) *skip out, fly the coop, make a break for it.*
- *dog cheap* (of little worth): (1) No; (2) *dirt cheap, peanuts, diddly, squat.*

- *funeral* (business): (1) Yes; (3) *Funeral* still has an idiomatic sense in phrases like *It's your funeral*, but instead of just meaning 'it's your business,' it means 'it's your business, but you're making a mistake.'
- *to get over* (seduce, fascinate): (1) Yes; (3) This now means 'recover from' as in *I'll get over it*.
- *groovy* (settled, limited): (1) Yes; (3) 'really good, great'; in modern slang usage, it is sometimes used jokingly and regarded as archaic (old slang).
- *grub* (food): (1) Yes.
- *head* (toilet, nautical use): (1) Yes; (3) No longer restricted to nautical use.
- *hook* (marry): (1) Yes; (2) *hitch* (as in *get hitched*); (3) It occurs in the phrase *hook up* which means 'to have sex with (outside of marriage).'
- *hump* (spoil): (1) Yes; (3) 'have or simulate sexual intercourse.'
- *hush money* (blackmail): (1) Yes.
- *itch* (be sexually excited): (1) Yes.
- *jam* (sweetheart): (1) No; (2) *baby, squeeze*; (3) 'unmoving traffic formation'; *jam* is now also a verb meaning 'go, leave, split.'
- *leg bags* (stockings): (1) No; (2) *nylons, hose*.
- *to lie low* (bide time): (1) Yes.
- *to lift a leg on* (have sexual intercourse): (1) No; (2) *get laid, get it on, do it, knock boots, bump uglies*.
- *looby* (a fool): (1) No; (2) *dork*.
- *malady of France* (syphilis): (1) No; (2) *clap, VD*.
- *nix* (nothing): (1) Yes; (3) This can mean 'nothing' or just 'no' (a negative command or answer).
- *noddle* (the head): (1) No; (2) *noodle, noggin, cabeza*.
- *old* (money): (1) No; (2) *bread, dough, bucks, moolah, cash*.
- *to pill* (talk platitudes): (1) Yes; (3) There is no slang expression that we know of that even comes close to the interpretation given. However, there is a slang noun *pill*, 'someone who is hard to get along with, a bother,' and the noun phrase *the pill*, which refers to birth control pills.
- *pipe layer* (political intriguer, schemer): (1) No; (2) There's no current equivalent that we know of, although one might suggest the noun *politicker*, the borrowed *politico*, or the verb phrase *play politics*.
- *poky* (cramped, stuffy, stupid): (1) Yes; (3) *poky* (or *pokey*) can also mean 'slow' or 'jail.'
- *pot* (quart, large sum, prize, urinal, excel): (1) Yes; (3) *pot* can still mean 'large sum' or 'communal money,' 'prize,' or 'urinal,' but not 'quart' or 'excel'; it can also mean 'marijuana.'
- *puny* (freshman): (1) Yes; (3) pejorative term meaning 'small.'
- *puss-gentleman* (effeminate): (1) No; (2) *nelly, queen, fag*.

**83**

4. *Slang dictionary.* Sample answers:
    1. *OMG*: Wow! (from Oh my God!)
    2. *chill*: cool down; stop acting excited, angry, or nervous
    3. *dog*: friend (between males)
    4. *pull an all-nighter*: stay up all night studying
    5. *catch some Zs*: get some sleep
    6. *hit the books*: study
    7. *mad*: very, as in *my class starts mad early*
    8. *ink*: a tattoo
    9. *bummed (out)*: unhappy, depressed
    10. *crash*: sleep in a particular place; a common aftereffect of drug intoxication

5. *British–American equivalents.*

| **British** | | **American** |
|---|---|---|
| a. | clothes peg | clothes pin |
| b. | braces | suspenders |
| c. | lift | elevator |
| d. | pram | baby buggy/stroller |
| e. | waistcoat | vest |
| f. | shop assistant | clerk |
| g. | sweets | candy |
| h. | boot (of a car) | trunk |
| i. | bobby | cop |
| j. | spanner | wrench |
| k. | biscuits | crackers |
| l. | queue | line |
| m. | torch | flashlight |
| n. | underground | subway |
| o. | high street | main street |
| p. | crisps | potato chips |
| q. | lorry | truck |
| r. | holiday | vacation |
| s. | tin | can |
| t. | knock up | wake up |

6. *Pig Latin.*

    A. (i)  Dialect 1: Suffix [me] to any vowel-initial word.
    Dialect 2: Suffix [he] to any vowel-initial word.
    Dialect 3: Suffix [e] to any vowel-initial word.

(ii) Phonetic transcriptions:

|  | Dialect 1 | Dialect 2 | Dialect 3 |
|---|---|---|---|
| honest | [anɪstme] | [anɪsthe] | [anɪste] |
| admire | [ædmaɪrme] | [ædmaɪrhe] | [ædmaɪre] |
| illegal | [ɪligɛlme] | [ɪligɛlhe] | [ɪligɛle] |

B. (i) Dialect 1: Take the onset (all initial consonants) from the first syllable of the word, add [e], and suffix the resulting syllable to the end of the word.

Dialect 2: Take only the first consonant from the first syllable of the word, add [e], and suffix the resulting syllable to the end of the word.

(ii) Phonetic transcriptions:

|  | Dialect 1 | Dialect 2 |
|---|---|---|
| spot | [atspe] | [patse] |
| crisis | [aɪsɪskre] | [raɪsɪske] |
| scratch | [ætʃskre] | [krætʃse] |

7. *Other English language games.*

   a. /aɪ tʊk maɪ dag aʊtsaɪd/ (I took my dog outside.)
      The rule is to suffix [o] to each syllable.

   b. /hir ɪz ə mɔr kamplɪketəd gem/ (Here is a more complicated game.)
      The rule is to suffix [li] after every syllable.

   c. Mary can talk in rhyme.
      The rule is to copy each word, replace the initial consonants of each copied word with [shm], or add initial [shm] if the word begins with a vowel, and suffix the newly formed word to the original.

   d. Better late than never.
      The rule is to copy each syllable, replace the initial consonants (if any) of each copied syllable with [p], and suffix the newly formed syllable to the original.

   e. The football stadium blew down.
      The rule is to insert -op- after the initial consonant(s) of each syllable, or prefix it if there is no syllable-initial consonant.

   f. /kæn ju spik ðɪs kaɪnd əv ɪŋglɪʃ/ (Can you speak this kind of English?)
      The rule is to insert the stressed syllable [ʌb] after the initial consonant(s) of each syllable or prefix it if there is no initial consonant.

8. *Informal English.*

   a. Where've ya been today? ← Where have you been today?
      Contraction of *where have* to *where've.*
      Use of *ya* for *you.*

   b. Watcha gonna do for fun? ← What are you going to do for fun? (or) What will you do for fun?

85

Contraction of *what are you* to *watcha*.
Substitution of less formal *are going to* for *will*.
Contraction of *going to* to *gonna*.

c. Him go to church? ← Does he go to church?
Auxiliary *does* is dropped.
Object pronoun *him* is substituted for subject pronoun *he*.

d. There's four books there. ← There are four books there.
Change of copula from plural *are* to singular *is*.
Contraction of *there is* to *there's*.

e. Who ya wanna go with? ← Who do you want to go with? (or) Whom do you want to go with? (or) With whom do you want to go?
Preposition not fronted.
Case ending on *who* dropped.
Auxiliary *do* is dropped.
Use of *ya* for *you*.
*Want to* contracted to *wanna*.

9. *Jargon.* Answers to this exercise will naturally vary according to the profession or trade the student chooses to represent. The jargon listed here as a sample answer is taken from the field of academic professors at the University of California, Los Angeles.

*chair*—the head of a department

*CV*—curriculum vitae, the academic résumé

*AA*—administrative assistant

*RA*—research assistant

*TA*—teaching assistant

*post-doc (post-doctoral)*—a temporary job (usually one to five years) in research or teaching for someone who has just completed a doctorate.

*ATC (Advanced to Candidacy)*—the level of a student who has finished all requirements for a Ph.D. except a dissertation.

*ABD (All But Dissertation)*—same as *ATC*.

*sabbatical*—paid leave of absence, originally after six years of teaching, i.e., the seventh year.

*FTE (Full-Time Equivalency)*—a full time academic position in the university.

10. *Formal-colloquial translation.* Here is a sample "translation" of the first paragraph of the Declaration of Independence. There are varying degrees of informality in style that could be used in doing this exercise.

*When a group of people wants to break away from another group and form their own country (which they should have the right to do), they've got to say clearly what motivated the separation, if they've got any respect for the opinion of the rest of the world.*

11. *Cockney rhyming slang.*

|   | A | B |
|---|---|---|
|   | **Rhyming Slang** | **Word** |
| a. | drip dry | cry |
| b. | in the mood | food |
| c. | insects and ants | pants |
| d. | orchestra stalls | balls |
| e. | Oxford scholar | dollar |
| f. | strike me dead | bread |
| g. | ship in full sail | ale |

*Constructed rhyming slang.* Sample answers:

| h. | chair | cut your hair |
|---|---|---|
| i. | house | dirty louse |
| j. | coat | around the moat |
| k. | eggs | eat the dregs |
| l. | pencil | window sill |

12. *Euphemisms.*

|   | A (Euphemism) | B (Meaning) |
|---|---|---|
| a. | Montezuma's revenge | diarrhea |
| b. | joy stick | penis |
| c. | friggin' | fuckin' |
| d. | ethnic cleansing | genocide |
| e. | French letter (old) | condom |
| f. | diddle oneself | masturbate |
| g. | holy of holies | vagina |
| h. | spend a penny (British) | urinate |
| i. | ladies' cloak room | women's toilet |
| j. | knock off (from 1919) | kill |
| k. | vertically challenged | short |
| l. | hand in one's dinner pail | die |
| m. | sanitation engineer | garbage collector |
| n. | downsize | fire |
| o. | peace keeping | waging war |

13. *Words which resemble derogatory words.* To argue against this statement, the student could note that there is nothing about the phonemes that a word is made up of that makes it derogatory or racist, so the fact that *niggardly* shares several phonemes with *nigger* does not mean that the negative connotations of *nigger* carry over to *niggardly*. The word *niggardly* has an entirely independent meaning that has nothing to do with race. Would we wish to ban the use of words such as *bigger* and *niggle* that also share phonemes in common with *nigger*? To defend the statement, the student would appeal to social sensitivity and the fact that *niggardly* is not

**87**

a common word and might easily be mistaken for an offensive word. This shows an awareness that language and culture are intermixed and inseparable on the social level, though the language faculty itself is fundamentally biological.

14. *Waitron and waitperson.* Answers will vary. A Google search retrieved 119,000 hits for *waitron* and 205,000 hits for *waitperson*. Thus, it appears that the latter is slightly more popular. Also, they both appear in the Merriam Webster online dictionary (http://www.merriam-webster.com/). The gender-specific word *waitress* generated 65 million hits and *waiter* retrieved 53,200,000. Clearly, *waitress* and *waiter* are used significantly more than *waitron* and *waitperson*, at least online. In light of the high frequency of these words, it may be that neither of the proposed replacements will succeed in gaining a foothold. An interesting alternative might be to consider whether *waiter* might be becoming a gender-neutral term. A Google search for the phrase "she is a waiter" retrieved 11.5 million hits, significantly more than either *waitron* or *waitperson*. "He is a waiter" returned 15 million hits. My prediction, then, is that *waiter* will become the gender-neutral term for a waiter or waitress.

A different point of view is available from the Google N-gram Viewer, which reports statistical results in print in books: Occurrences are: Waiter = 45/million (words) in 1940; 25/million in 2000. *Waitress* = 1/million in 1940; 17/million in 2000. *Wait person* = 0 in 1940; .00012/million in 2000. *Waitron* = 0 in 1940; .00026/million in 2000. As in all scientific endeavors—and sociolinguistics is science—results at first often conflict, and their significance and ramifications must be weighed carefully.

15. *Tok Pisin.* Answers will vary.

16. *Language game.*
    Cogito ergo sum.
    foreplay
    Veni, vidi, vici.
    graffiti
    ignoramus
    rigor mortis (Morris was a cat used in TV advertising in the past.)
    feliz navidad (Spanish for 'merry Christmas')
    Veni, vidi, vici.
    libido
    haute cuisine
    L'etat, c'est moi
    intoxication
    ex post facto
    Answers for new examples will vary. For instance, *bite the mullet*, from *bite the bullet*, meaning 'eat your fish.'

17. *Newspeak.* Answers will vary. It is unlikely that Newspeak would achieve its goal. Human languages permit virtually infinite creativity regardless of the content of their lexicons. Thousands of traditional languages are still in use in rapidly modernizing societies, despite the fact that until recently their lexicons did not include words for many of the objects or concepts of modern life.

18. *Nameless concepts.* Answers will vary. What this notion misses is that the concepts humans can entertain are not limited by the words in their lexicons. So long as there is syntax (and/or morphology), words can be combined, and an infinite number of new concepts can be conceived and discussed. New words can also be invented or borrowed to name such "nameless" concepts.

19. *Gender and lexical choice.* Answers will vary. One observation commonly made is that women use uncommon color terms such as *mauve* or *beige* more frequently then men. Men tend to use more "four-letter" words than women, especially ones that denigrate women.

20. *Banned languages.* Answers will vary. For example, Macedonian was once banned in Greece.

21. *Abbreviated English.*
    A. Translations.
       a. Clinton **is** in Bulgaria this week.
       b. **An** old man **has** found **a** rare coin.
       c. Bush **has** hired **his** wife as secretary.
       d. **The** pope **has** died in **the** Vatican.
    B. Distinguishing features of AE.
       Some distinguishing features include the obligatory omission of the copula (forms of *to be*), indefinite and definite articles, and possessive pronouns, and the use of present tense to have a perfective interpretation rather than the typical habitual one.
    C. Other contexts (answers may vary).
       Recipes and journals exhibit similar—but not identical—abbreviated forms. Recipes are generally series of orders, so there is a dropped (but implied) second-person subject with concomitant verb agreement (place flour in bowl; stir thoroughly, mix with water . . .). It would not be incorrect to say that the auxiliary *should* is also dropped ((you) (should) place flour in bowl). Notice that determiners can also be dropped in recipes, as with *(the) bowl* above.

       Journal and diary writing may feature a dropped (but implied) first-person subject (went to office early—wrote memo to self—came home on bus, etc.) As with recipes, articles may be dropped (*went to (the) office early*) in journal writing; and in both genres, some third-person

**89**

pronouns may be omitted (*mix (it) with water*). However, recipes and journal writing do not feature the simple present with perfective interpretation, which is typical of newspaper headlines.

*Challenge exercises:*

D. The time reference in the Clinton example is present; for the other three, the time reference is past.

E. Statives tend to get a present-tense interpretation; eventives tend to get a perfective interpretation.

22. *Euphemisms in daytime soaps.* Answers will vary.

23. *That's not a language, it's a dialect.* Answers will vary. Here is one possible retort: It's interesting that you use *dialect* in that way because linguists actually use it differently. I've heard a lot of people use *dialect* to refer to languages that don't have much social prestige, like indigenous languages or languages without writing systems. But I learned that all languages are equally languages, whether or not they have social prestige or are spoken by a group of people that are politically under-represented, or are written, etc. There is no language that is just a dialect. Linguists use the word *dialect* to mean something different, namely, a language variety. For example, English has many dialects: the dialect spoken in Southern California is different from the dialect spoken in Massachusetts, but they are both varieties of English and can be called dialects of American English. What you are speaking right now, for example, is a dialect.

24. *Preserving linguistic diversity.* Answers will vary. Sample answer: A society can act to preserve linguistic diversity by promoting multiple language use. This can be done by setting up cultural/language centers that also act as social clubs. The society might also promote the use of nonstandard languages by strengthening economic and social ties with countries in which the nonstandard languages are spoken. Giving equal political weight to the nonstandard languages is another way to promote multiple language use. In this way, the nonstandard language is seen as an important tool in interacting in the community at its highest level, that of the government. Here are three additional possible ways to encourage endangered language use in a community: 1. Set up low-cost or free target language immersion preschools; 2. Allow foreign language credit for fluency in the target language at a high school or college level; 3. Have an annual poetry writing contest in the target language. Have real prizes and public reading of the poems and awarding of the prizes.

25. *Ebonics in the classroom.* Answers will vary. Possible arguments in favor of the use of Ebonics in the classroom include that the use of Ebonics in a classroom would make the students who are speakers of this variety feel more respected and comfortable and this promotes an atmosphere

of learning and more open communication between the students and the teachers. Another argument is that teaching important subjects like geography or science in the students' native dialect may help them learn those subjects more readily. Possible arguments against the use of Ebonics in the classroom include that encouraging the use of a non-prestige variety of English could actually hurt speakers of this variety in the future, limiting their advancement academically and stymying their career potential. The idea here is that it is better for the students who are speakers of Ebonics to become bi-dialectal and learn the standard English dialect for use in school and professionally.

26. *The use of Karen in Myanmar.* Answers will vary.

27. *Pygmalion.* Answers will vary. Professor Henry Higgins would benefit from an introductory linguistics class. His notion that only foreigners who have been explicitly taught the rules of English can speak it well is clearly coming from a notion of prescriptive grammar. His claim that "the English do not know how to speak their own language" would be laughable to a linguist. All native speakers of a language can speak their language! Henry Higgins, in addition to being a prescriptivist, seems to think that some dialects of a language are less prestigious than others. It is likely that he thinks everyone should speak the "proper" way, i.e., using the prestige dialect. He seems to judge use of other dialects of English as a lack of knowledge of the language—rather than knowledge of another language variety.

# Chapter 8

1. *Old English sound changes.*

|  | | **Change(s)** |
|---|---|---|
| a. crabba [kraba] → crab | | 1. The vowel [a] became [æ]. |
| | | 2. The word-final [a] was lost. |
| b. fisc [fɪsk] → fish | | 1. The [s] became [ʃ]. |
| | | 2. The final [k] was lost. |
| c. fūl [fuːl] → foul | | 1. The long vowel [uː] became [aʊ]. |
| d. gāt [gaːt] → goat | | 1. The long vowel [aː] became [o]. |
| e. lǣfan [læːvan] → leave | | 1. The long vowel [æː] became [i]. |
| | | 2. The [an] ending was lost. |
| f. teþ [teːθ] → teeth | | 1. The long vowel [eː] became [i]. |

2. *Great vowel shift.* Answers will vary. Sample answers:

| [i]/[ɛ] | [aɪ]/[ɪ] | [e]/[æ] |
|---|---|---|
| a. clean/cleanse | deride/derision | vain/vanity |
| b. thief/theft | rhyme/rhythm | sate/satisfy |
| c. feel/felt | crime/criminal | flame/flammable |
| d. keep/kept | precise/precision | nation/national |
| e. please/pleasure | line/linear | page/paginate |

3. *Changes in English.* In the answers given below, only syntactic changes are discussed. Lexical changes (e.g., *hath* to *has*) are not noted.

   a. <u>It</u> nothing pleased his master.

   ModE (Modern English): Nothing pleased his master.

   Change: In Old English (OE) the expletive subject *it* co-occurred with the logical subject (in this case, *nothing*). In ModE this is not possible: expletive *it* appears only when there is no other subject available.

   b. He ha<u>th</u> said that we would lift <u>them whom that him please</u>.

   ModE: He has said that we would lift those who please him.

   Change: 1. In OE, pronouns like *them* can take a relative clause, while in ModE they generally cannot—they are replaced in ModE by demonstratives like *those*. 2. In OE the *wh* phrase *whom* and the complementizer *that* both occurred in the complementizer position, while in ModE only one of them may occur there. 3. In OE the object *him* can go before the verb *please*, while in ModE the verb must precede the object.

c. I have a brother _____ is condemned to die.
　　ModE: I have a brother who is condemned to die.
　　Change: It appears that in OE a relative pronoun (the pronoun occurring in the complementizer of a relative clause) corresponding to the subject of the relative clause may be null. In ModE a subject relative pronoun cannot be null.

d. I bade them _____ take <u>away you</u>.
　　ModE: I asked them to take you away.
　　Change: In OE a verb-particle pair could be followed by a pronoun. In ModE if the verb and the particle are separable, the particle must follow the object if the object is a pronoun. Additionally, ModE would require a *to* before *take*.

e. I wish you <u>was still</u> more _____ a Tartar.
　　ModE: I wish you were even more of a Tartar / I wish even more that you were a Tartar.
　　Change: 1. The verb *be* must agree in ModE with the subject.
　　　　　　　2. Depending on what the meaning is interpreted to be, either *of* must be inserted into the phrase *more a Tartar* because *more* cannot modify a predicate nominal in ModE; or the phrase *still more*, modifying *wish*, must precede the embedded sentence.

f. Christ slept and his apostles _____.
　　ModE: Christ slept and his apostles did too.
　　Change: In OE a verb phrase could be entirely missing if identical to the preceding verb phrase. In ModE an auxiliary verb (*did* in this case) must remain.

g. <u>Me</u> was told.
　　ModE: I was told.
　　Change: In OE the subject of a passive clause appeared with accusative case, while in ModE it must have nominative case.

4. *Recent and archaic words in English.* Answers will vary. Sample answers:
　a. 1. *fronting*: putting on a front that you are something you're not or have something you don't.
　　　2. *bromance*: an especially close friendship between two men. From *bro* (clipped from *brother*) + *romance*.
　　　3. *occupy*: from the "occupy Wall Street" movement in 2011, but which took on it's own life and can now be used as a noun, verb, or in other compounds such as *Occupy TV*. (This was the voted the Word of the Year by the American Dialect Society in 2011.)
　　　4. *cloud* or *in the cloud*: the use of online space for storage or processing.
　　　5. *app*: an application for a smart phone or tablet computer. (This was the voted the Word of the Year by the American Dialect Society in 2010.)

b. 1. *slide rule*: a handheld instrument the size of a foot-long ruler used to calculate square roots and other mathematical relations; fast becoming obsolete with the advances of computer technology.
   2. *phonograph*: record player, turntable.
   3. *floppy disk*: this was a recent word in the fifth edition of this book. With floppy disk drives now becoming more obsolete, this term is fast fading from the language.
   4. *icebox*: refrigerator; now nearly obsolete since ice hasn't been used to refrigerate for decades.
c. 1. *credit card* meaning 'to buy with a credit card', e.g., I can't really afford this, but I'm just going to credit card it.
   2. *trend* meaning 'to be popular on twitter', e.g., McKayla Maroney's near perfect vault is trending like crazy.
   3. *timeline* meaning 'to produce a schedule of subgoals for a task', e.g., We'll need to timeline the project.
d. 1. *sextant*: Once used for navigation, it is now becoming obsolete with the advent of electronic positioning systems and computerized sky charts.
   2. *rural free delivery*: Once used to express the special attention given to rural areas by the U.S. Postal Service but now obsolete due to improved transportation technology. (Note: though it appears to consist of three words, it is really a single compound word.)
   3. *shortwave*: Special radio waves that traveled a long distance by reflecting off the ionosphere, now becoming obsolete owing to satellite communications.
   4. *phaeton*: A light, four-wheeled open carriage, usually drawn by a pair of horses. Need we say more?
e. Answers will vary.
   1. *PowerToy* from Microsoft. "PowerToys are additional programs that developers work on after a product has been released." (from http://www.microsoft.com/windowsxp/Downloads/powertoys/Xppowertoys.mspx)
   2. *PowerReporting*. Website on resources for journalists. (http://www.powerreporting.com/)
   3. *Power Proofreading*. An educational website for children. (http://www.eduplace.com/kids/hme/k_5/proofread/proof.htm)
   4. *PowerBar*. 'a brand of bar-shaped food intended for use esp. by athletes, having a high carbohydrate and low fat content with protein and vitamin supplements.' (from dictionary.reference.com)
   5. *power broker*. 'a person who wields great political, governmental, or financial power.' (from dictionary.reference.com)
f. Answers will vary.
   1. *blogzilla*. A blogger who goes easily loses his/her temper and goes off on rants.
   2. *pre-blog*. To blog about an event before it happens.

3. *blogosphere*. The blogging world; the set of all blogs.

4. *blogonomics*. The study of how information is traded on blogs.

5. *Latin–French correspondences.*

   a. False. The modern French word for 'thing' shows that a /k/, which occurred before the vowel /a/ in Latin, became [ʃ] in French.

   b. True. As *kor* → *kœr* 'heart' shows us, /k/ before /o/ in Latin remains a /k/ in modern French. But *kawsa* → ʃoz 'thing' shows us that /k/ before /aw/ in Latin changes to a /ʃ/. Since the modern French word for 'tail' starts with a /k/, we would predict that it did not derive from a Latin word that started with *kaw* because then we would expect the modern French word to start with a /ʃ/.

   c. False. The modern French words [kã] 'when' and [sã] 'hundred' show that [s] is not an allophone of /k/ in modern French, but rather a distinct phoneme.

   d. True. We have evidence that Latin *kervus* became modern French [sɛr], so a change of *kertus* to [sɛr] seems probable, since the *k* is in the same phonetic environment (before the [e]).

6. *Indo-European.* The Indo-European languages are the ones numbered 1, 2, 4, 8, 10, and 11.

7. *Etymology.* The answers below come from the *Random House Dictionary of the English Language*, 2nd edition (unabridged). Only the etymological information associated with each word is given below; the student may speculate freely on how each word was borrowed.

   a. *size*: From Old French *assiser* ('assize'), which has as one of its meanings 'a statute for regulating weights and measures.'

   b. *royal*: From Middle French from Latin *regalis* ('kingly').

   c. *aquatic*: From Middle French from Latin *aqua* ('water') + *-aticus*.

   d. *heavenly*: From OE *heofenlic*; akin to Old Norse *himinn*; Goth *himins*; German *Himmel*.

   e. *skill*: From Old Norse *skil* ('distinction, difference').

   f. *ranch*: From Spanish *rancho* ('camp').

   g. *blouse*: From French *vêtement de laine blouse* ('garment of short (uncarded) wool').

   h. *robot*: From Czech, coined by Karel Capek in the play *R.U.R.* (1920) from the base *robot-*, as in *robota* ('compulsory labor'), *robotnik* ('peasant owing such labor').

   i. *check*: From Old French *eschec*, var. of *eschac* from Arabic *shah* ('check') (in chess); from Persian: lit., *king* (an exclamation: i.e., "look out, your king is threatened.")

   j. *banana*: From Portuguese (perhaps via Spanish); akin to various words for banana or plantain in West African languages (e.g., Wolof, Malinke *banana*; Vai *bana*), but ultimate source and direction of borrowing uncertain.

k. *keel*: From OE *ceol*, from Gothic *kiel* ('ship').

l. *fact*: From Latin *factum* ('something done, deed').

m. *potato*: From Spanish *patata* ('white potato'), var. of *batata* ('sweet potato'), from Taino.

n. *muskrat*: Alteration by folk etymology of *musquash*, Massachusett cognate of Western Abenaki *mòskwas*.

o. *coyote*: From the Nahuatl *coyotl*, borrowed through Spanish.

p. *chocolate*: From Nahuatl *xocolatl*, which probably meant 'bitter water', borrowed through Spanish.

q. *hoodlum*: probably from dialectal German; cf. Swabian derivatives of *Hudel* ('rag'), e.g., *hudelum* ('disorderly'), *hudellam* ('weak,' 'slack,' etc.).

r. *filibuster*: From Spanish *filibustero* from Middle French *flibustier*, var. of *fribustier*; see FREEBOOTER.

s. *astronaut*: From French *astronautique* ASTRO + *-naute* from Greek *naútes* ('sailor'), on the model of *aéronaute* ('aeronaut').

t. *emerald*: From Old French *esmeraude, esmeralde, esmeragde*, from Latin *smaragdus*, from Greek *smáragdos*; probably ultimately from Semitic *b-r-q* ('shine') Sanskrit *marak(a)la* ('emerald').

u. *sugar*: From Middle English and Middle French *sucre*, from Middle Latin *succarum*, Italian *zucchero*, Arabic *sukkar*; obscurely akin to Persian *shakar*, Greek *sákcharon*.

v. *pagoda*: From Portuguese *pagode* 'temple', from Persian *butkada*— *but* 'idol' + *kada* 'temple, dwelling'.

w. *khaki*: From Urdu, from Persian *khaki* ('dusty'), equivalent to *khak* ('dust') + *i* (suffix of appurtenance).

x. *shampoo*: Earlier *champo* ('to massage'), from an inflected form of Hindi *campna* (lit., 'to press').

y. *kangaroo*: From Guugu Yimidhirr (Australian Aboriginal language spoken around Cooktown, N. Queensland) /gaN-urru/ 'large black or gray species of kangaroo'.

z. *tomato*: from Nahuatl *tomatl* 'tomato', borrowed through Spanish.

8. *Analogic change.* Sample answers:

1. In common usage, it is considered nonstandard to say *it's me, I'm her*, etc., as opposed to *it is I* or *I am she*. In standard English, pronouns in the accusative case form are typically in a non-initial position in a sentence, while subject pronouns (which are in the nominative case form) are usually initial. Speakers for whom *it's me* is well-formed have generalized (or reinterpreted) the distinction of *subject* vs. *object* to one of *initial* vs. *non-initial*.

2. In standard English, *you* can be either singular or plural. "Tim saw you" can mean that Tim saw one person or more than one person. However, some speakers have extended the *-s* plural of English to be used with this pronoun. For these speakers, "Tim saw you" can only describe Tim seeing one person. "Tim saw yous" (pronounced [juz]) would refer to Tim seeing more than one person.

3. Verbs in English typically fall into two categories: (1) verbs where the past tense and the past participle are the same (examples: "I sit." "I sat." "I have sat.") (2) verbs where there are three distinct forms (examples: "I see." "I saw." "I have seen."). Some speakers have generalized the pattern seen in Type 1 to the verbs of Type 2. For example: "I see." "I seen." "I have seen."

9. *Regularity and irregularity.* Sound change is regular because every affected sound in a particular environment is changed to another sound. For example, the Great Vowel Shift in English *regularly* caused all [iː]s to become the diphthong [aɪ]. This change, together with the Early Middle English Vowel Shorting Rule, created an *irregularity* in lexical pairs such as *divine/divinity*. Analogical change, in contrast, is not regular. It does not affect all the sounds in a particular environment. Rather, the change is irregular, affecting only certain words and in non-regular ways, such as *kine → cows*. But while the change itself is irregular, it creates more morphological regularity. For example, *cows* follows a regular morphological rule for creating the plural from *cow*, while *kine* did not.

10. *The English of* Hamlet.

    Line 1: *hath eat of a king* is now *has eaten a king.*

    Line 1: *eat of the fish* is now *eat the fish.*

    Line 2: *hath fed of that worm* is now *has fed on that worm.*

    Line 3: *what dost thou* is now *what do you.*

    Line 4: *may go a progress* is now *may progress.*

    Line 7: *send thither* is now *send someone there.*

    Line 7: *if your messenger find him not* is now *if your messenger does not find him.*

    Line 8: *i'* is no longer contractible and is now *in.*

    Line 8: *if you find him not* is now *if you do not find him.*

    Line 9: *you shall*, with the same meaning, is now *you will.*

    Line 9: *nose* as a verb with the same meaning is now *smell.*

11. *Spanish dialects.*

    a. Correspondence sets:
      i.    k-k
      ii.   a-a

iii.  s-θ
iv.  s-s
v.  i-i
vi.  g-g
vii.  j-ʎ
viii.  o-o
ix.  d-d
x.  e-e
xi.  p-p
xii.  j-j
xiii.  m-m
xiv.  ŋ-ŋ

b. Protosounds:
  i.  k-k *k
  ii.  a-a *a
  iii.  s-θ *θ
  iv.  s-s *s
  v.  i-i *i
  vi.  g-g *g
  vii.  j-ʎ *ʎ
  viii.  o-o *o
  ix.  d-d *d
  x.  e-e *e
  xi.  p-p *p
  xii.  j-j *j
  xiii.  m-m *m
  xiv.  ŋ-ŋ *ŋ

c.

| | |
|---|---|
| Dialect 1: | *[ʎ] → [j] |
| | and *[θ] → [s] |
| Dialect 2: | none |

d.

| Dialect 1 | Dialect 2 | Gloss | Earlier Form |
|---|---|---|---|
| [kasa] | [kaθa] | hunt (noun) | *[kasa] |
| [si] | [si] | yes | *[si] |
| [gajo] | [gaʎo] | rooster | *[gaʎo] |
| [dies] | [dieθ] | ten | *[dieθ] |
| [pojo] | [pojo] | kind of bench | *[pojo] |
| [kaje] | [kaʎe] | street | *[kaʎe] |
| [majo] | [majo] | May | *[majo] |
| [kasa] | [kasa] | house | *[kasa] |
| [siŋko] | [θiŋko] | five | *[θiŋko] |
| [dos] | [dos] | two | *[dos] |
| [pojo] | [poʎo] | chicken | *[poʎo] |

12. *Proto-Polynesian.*

    a. Correspondence sets:

      i.     p-p-p-b
      ii.    o-o-o-o
      iii.   u-u-u-u
      iv.   t-k-t-t
      v.    a-a-a-a
      vi.   ŋ-n-ŋ-ŋ
      vii.  i-i-i-i
      viii. k-ʔ-ʔ-k
      ix.   e-e-e-e
      x.    r-l-l-l
      xi.   h-h-f-v
      xii.  n-n-n-n
      xiii. m-m-m-m
      xiv. h-h-s-s

    b. Protosounds:

| | | | |
|---|---|---|---|
| i. | p-p-p-b | *p | p → b in Fijian |
| ii. | o-o-o-o | *o | |
| iii. | u-u-u-u | *u | |
| iv. | t-k-t-t | *t | t → k in Hawaiian |
| v. | a-a-a-a | *a | |
| vi. | ŋ-n-ŋ-ŋ | *ŋ | ŋ → n in Hawaiian |
| vii. | i-i-i-i | *i | |
| viii. | k-ʔ-ʔ-k | *ʔ | ʔ → k in Maori and Fijian |
| ix. | e-e-e-e | *e | |
| x. | r-l-l-l | *l | l → r in Maori |
| xi. | h-h-f-v | *f | f → h in Maori and Hawaiian |
| | | | f → v in Fijian |
| xii. | n-n-n-n | *n | |
| xiii. | m-m-m-m | *m | |
| xiv. | h-h-s-s | *s | s → h in Maori and Hawaiian |

    c. Reconstructed words in Proto-Polynesian. These proto forms are the same as in Samoan.

      *pou
      *tapu
      *taŋi
      *taʔele
      *fono
      *malama
      *ʔaso

13. *Reconstruction of American Indian languages.*

a. Correspondence sets:

| Consonants | | Vowels | |
|---|---|---|---|
| i. | m-m | i. | u-u |
| ii. | p-p | ii. | i-i |
| iii. | t-t | iii. | a-a |
| iv. | m-w | iv. | ɨ-ɨ |
| v. | w-w | v. | o-o |
| vi. | s-s | vi. | a-e |
| vii. | ʔ-ʔ | | |
| viii. | n-n | | |
| ix. | h-h | | |
| x. | k-k | | |

b. Protosounds:

(1) Reconstruction:

| p-p | *p | u-u | *u |
|---|---|---|---|
| t-t | *t | i-i | *i |
| s-s | *s | a-a | *a |
| ʔ-ʔ | *ʔ | ɨ-ɨ | *ɨ |
| n-n | *n | o-o | *o |
| h-h | *h | a-e | *e |
| k-k | *k | | |

(2) The only protosound listed above that underwent a change is *e, which became *a* in Yerington Paviotso.

c. (1) Whenever a *w* appears in Yerington Paviotso, the sound in the corresponding position in Northfork Monachi is also *w*.

(2) Whenever an *m* occurs in Yerington Paviotso, the two sounds that may correspond to it in Northfork Monachi are *m* or *w*.

(3) Yes, the correspondence is predictable. An *m* in Yerington Paviotso corresponds to an *m* in Northfork Monachi word-initially, and a *w* in Northfork Monachi between vowels.

d. (1) Two protosounds should be reconstructed.

(2) If you chose three, they would have to be *m, *w, and an abstract sound representing both of them, perhaps *b. Then *m corresponds to *m* in both languages, *w corresponds to *w* in both languages, and *b corresponds to *m* word-initially and *w* between vowels in Northfork Monachi. But this solution is unmotivated; the simpler solution below is better.

(3) The protosounds are *m and *w. Proto *m becomes *m* in Yerington Paviotso. In Northfork Monachi, proto *m becomes *m* word-initially and *w* between vowels. Proto *w becomes *w* in both Yerington Paviotso and Northfork Monachi.

e. The proto forms are the same as those in Yerington Paviotso except for the words with a proto *e sound.

| | |
|---|---|
| 'nose' | *mupi |
| 'tooth' | *tama |
| 'heart' | *piwɨ |
| 'a feminine name' | *sawaʔpono |
| 'liver' | *nɨmɨ |
| 'springtime' | *tamano |
| 'aunt' | *pahwa |
| 'husband' | *kuma |
| 'Indians living to the west' | *wowaʔa |
| 'porcupine' | *mɨhɨ |
| 'throat' | *noto |
| 'sun' | *tape |
| 'jaw' | *ʔatapɨ |
| 'older brother' | *papiʔi |
| 'daughter' | *peti |
| 'man' | *nana |
| 'bow,' 'gun' | *ʔetɨ |

14. *Proto-Egglish.*

  a. Correspondence sets:

    i.   ʃ-k
    ii.  u-u
    iii.  r-l
    iv.  v-v
    v.   e-e
    vi.  Ø-t
    vii.  r-r
    viii. ɔ-ɔ
    ix.  Ø-k
    x.   ʒ-g
    xi.  Ø-p
    xii.  l-l
    xiii. p-p

*Proto-Egglish words from which the cognates descended:*

| | |
|---|---|
| *kur | 'omelet' |
| *vet | 'yoke' |
| *rɔk | 'egg' |
| *ver | 'egg shell' |
| *gup | 'soufflé' |
| *vel | 'egg white' |
| *pe | 'hard-boiled' |

b. Sound changes.
i. velar stops → palatal fricatives, word-initially, in Big-End Egglish. This sound change is more likely than the opposite, because a change similar to this took place in French, as discussed earlier in the chapter. It is possible that this change is also conditioned by the high back vowel, so that the rule is velar stops → palatal fricatives word-initially before /u/, or possibly even before /u/ in non-final position. The data are insufficient to determine this.
ii. voiceless stops → Ø, word-finally, in Big-End Egglish. There are no final voiced stops in the data set, so we cannot determine whether voiced stops underwent the same change. However, the more general statement that stops were deleted word-finally would also be acceptable.
iii. r → l, word-finally, in Little-End Egglish.

15. *Greek and Latin roots.* Answers will vary.
   *Greek*
   a. pente 'five': English *pentagram, pentagon, pentacle*
   b. anthropos 'man': English *anthropology, anthropomorphic, anthropogenic*
   c. arche 'beginning': English *archaic, archaeology, archetype*
   d. pathos 'feeling': English *empathy, sympathy, pathetic*
   e. morphe 'shape': English *anthropomorphic, morphology, morphed*
   f. exo 'outside': English *exoskeleton, exogamy, exorcism*
   g. sophos 'wise': English *philosophy, sophomore, sophist*
   h. gamos 'marriage': English *exogamy, gamete, bigamy*
   i. logy 'word': English *analogy, logarithm, logo*
   j. gigas 'huge, enormous': English *gigantic, gigabyte, giant*

   *Latin*
   k. acer 'sharp': English *acrimonious, acerbic, acrid*
   l. mater 'mother': English *maternal, matriarchy, matricide*
   m. bellum 'war': English *rebel, belligerent, bellicose*
   n. arbor 'tree': English *arboretum, arbor, arboreal*
   o. positus 'put, place': English *position, dispose, transpose*
   p. par 'equal': English *parity, pair, compare*
   q. nepos 'grandson': English *nepotism, nephew, nepotal*
   r. tacere 'to be silent': English *tacit, taciturn, tacitness*
   s. scribere 'to write': English *scribe, script, scribble*
   t. lingua 'tongue, language': English *linguistics, language, lingual*

16. *Post-nominal adjectives in English.*

   a. All the adjectives that occur post-nominally in data begin with *a-* and are related to a form that does not have the *a-*; i.e., the *a-* seems to be a morpheme.

   b. Other examples include:

      i. *aglow*: her face aglow / *her aglow face / her glowing face

      ii. *afloat*: a boat afloat / *an afloat boat / a floating boat

   c. Yes, the expressions in column C have the same meaning as their respective items in column A.

# Chapter 9

1. *Baby talk*. Individual answers will vary. The following are some suggestions for English.

   a. Semantic categories:
      Animals: horsey, kitty, piggy, bunny, doggie
      Events: bye-bye, night-night, boo-boo, ow-ow
      People: mama, dada, nana
      Objects: choo-choo, jammies, tummy, potty

   b. Rules:
      i. A consonant cluster may be reduced: for example, *stomach* [stʌmək] becomes *tummy* [tʌmi]; final consonants may be dropped.
      ii. Unstressed syllables may be dropped: for example [pədʒǽməz] becomes [dʒǽmiz].
      iii. The diminutive *-i* (spelled *y* or *ie*) may be suffixed to a word, sometimes replacing existing syllables.
      iv. Reduplicated syllables may also replace existing syllables, as in *bye-bye* for *good-bye*.

2. *Question formation*. In this stage, the child appears to be able to correctly form questions from positive statements, evidenced by *Can I go?*, *Why do you have one tooth?* and so on. However, the child is not forming negative questions correctly. Instead of inverting the subject and the negative auxiliary, the child is inserting a positive auxiliary to the left of the subject, while leaving the negative auxiliary in place. For example, from the statement *I can't go*, the question should be formed by inverting the subject and the negative auxiliary: *Can't I go?* But the child simply inserts the positive auxiliary *can*, coming up with *Can I can't go?* The utterance *Why you don't have a tongue?* is a little different because no positive auxiliary has been inserted. Rather, the negative auxiliary has been left in place instead of being inverted.

3. *A child's grammar*. Answers will vary according to the child, the language, the age, and the circumstances.

4. *"Two-word stage" grammar*.
   - *\*a celery*: *celery* is a noncount noun. You cannot say *\*one celery*, *\*five celeries* in English. One would have to say *one stalk* or *a bunch of celery* or *five stalks*. The determiner *a* can only be followed by single, countable nouns.

**104**

- *a Becky: Names, especially names of people, do not usually occur with determiners. However, note that this phrase is well-formed in certain contexts. For example: *My name is Becky, and I live next door to a Becky* (someone whose name is also Becky).
- *a hands: the article *a* must be followed by a singular noun.
- *more nut: *more* must be followed by a mass noun (*coffee*) or a plural noun (*nuts*).
- *two tinkertoy: numerals greater than one must be followed by a plural (and countable) noun.
- *that Adam: names don't usually occur with determiners, but the phrase may be well-formed in certain contexts: e.g., *That Adam is a charming boy.*

5. *Holophrastic stage phonology.*
   A. (Data given in phonetic transcription)

   | | | |
   |---|---|---|
   | (1) dõnt | dot | the final cluster [nt] reduced to single [t]; vowel not nasalized |
   | (2) skɪp | kʰɪp | initial cluster [sk] reduced to single consonant; [k] aspirated |
   | (3) ʃu | su | a palatal fricative is replaced by an alveolar fricative |
   | (4) ðæt | dæt | an interdental fricative is replaced by an alveolar stop |
   | (5) pʰle | pʰe | the initial cluster [pʰl] is replaced by a single aspirated stop |
   | (6) θʌ̃mp | dʌp | an initial voiceless interdental fricative is replaced by a voiced alveolar stop; the final [mp] cluster is replaced by the single [p]; the vowel is not nasalized |
   | (7) bæθ | bæt | a final interdental fricative is replaced by a voiceless alveolar stop |
   | (8) tʃap | tʰap | a palatal affricate is replaced by an alveolar stop; [t] is aspirated |
   | (9) kɪɾi | kɪdi | flap replaced by alveolar stop |
   | (10) laɪt | waɪt | lateral liquid replaced by (labio)velar glide |
   | (11) dali | dawi | lateral liquid replaced by (labio)velar glide |
   | (12) gro | go | initial cluster [gr] reduced to single consonant |

   B. General rules for children's pronunciation. Sample answer:
   - In consonant clusters consisting of a stop and a fricative, liquid, or nasal, delete the fricative, liquid, or nasal.
   - Replace interdental fricatives with alveolar stops. Voicing seems to be determined by the following rule: the stop is voiced word-initially and voiceless word-finally.

- Replace palatals with alveolars.
- Replace the lateral liquid with the (labio)velar glide.
- Replace the flap with the voiced alveolar stop.

6. *Acquisition of deixis.* As discussed in Chapter 4, these words are deictic words. Their meaning is dependent on the context of the utterance in which they occur (i.e., when and where the conversation takes place, the location of the speaker and the hearer, etc.). Children may have difficulty acquiring deictic expressions because their interpretation requires contextual information and their meaning changes depending on the circumstances of the utterance.

7. *Overgeneralization.*
   a. children—childs
   b. went—goed
   c. better—gooder
   d. best—goodest
   e. brought—bringed
   f. sang—singed
   g. geese—gooses
   h. worst—baddest
   i. knives—knifes
   j. worse—badder

8. *Child phonology.*
   a. Child 1 deletes final voiced stops (exemplified by *bib*, *slide*, and *dog*), but retains final voiceless stops (*soap, feet, sock*). The voiced fricative [z] is devoiced to [s] in this child's pronunciations of *cheese* and *shoes*. Also, the voiceless fricative [ʃ] is replaced with the affricate [tʃ] in *dish*.

   Child 2 appears to devoice all final consonants. An exception is *bead*, where the final [d] is deleted instead of being devoiced; the vowel is lengthened. Also, the final palatal fricative of *fish* has its place of articulation changed to alveolar.

   For both children, the classes of sounds that undergo the rules (voiced stops for child 1, all stops for child 2) constitute natural classes.

   b. Child 1 has one minimal pair: [daɪ] 'slide' and [da] 'dog', which show that /aɪ/ and /a/ contrast in his grammar. Child 2 has one minimal set containing three words: [gis] 'geese', [tis] 'cheese' and [bis] 'bees' showing that /g/, /t/, and /b/ are all distinct phonemes in the child's grammar.

9. *Wug tests.* Answers will vary but should be along the lines of the following: The child's knowledge of the comparative -*er* could be tested by showing her a picture of a boy with spotted skin. The researcher would say

"Look at this boy. His skin is really *wug*." Then the child could be shown another boy with even spottier skin. The researcher would say "Look at this boy. Look at his skin! His skin is even . . ." If the right intonation was used, the child would hopefully finish the sentence with *wugger.*

The superlative *-est* could be tested by showing a third boy with even more spotty skin and saying "Look at this boy. Look at his skin! His skin is the . . ." Again, intonation would be crucial in encouraging the child to complete the sentence with the superlative.

The present progressive could be tested by showing the child a doll and saying "Look at this doll! I'm going to make her *blick!*" The researcher would then make the doll perform some novel action such as spinning on one leg. The researcher would then ask the child, "What's she doing now?" The child would hopefully respond, "She's blicking."

The agentive could be tested with the same doll and action. The researcher could say, "This doll really likes to *blick*. She does it all the time. She's a really good . . ." With the right intonation, the child should finish the sentence with *blicker.*

10. *Overgeneralized argument structures.*

   a. In each of these five examples, the child has created a novel causative verb. In the first three examples, verbs that are intransitive in the sense intended have been used as if they were transitive, and in the last two examples, the causative verbs have been derived from adjectives. Although there are many similar causative alternations in English, creating causative verbs out of intransitive verbs and adjectives is not a fully productive process. It is possible that the children's grammar differs from the adult grammar in that they have not learned to restrict this rule.

   b. Similar but well-formed examples in adult English include:
   I broke the glass. (cf. The glass broke.)
   The baby toppled the tower of blocks. (cf. The tower of blocks toppled.)
   I cleaned the table. (cf. The table is clean.)

11. *Egyptian and Iraqi Arabic.*

   a. Egyptian Arabic speakers insert a high front vowel [i]. It is inserted between two consonants that start a syllable (i.e., comprise the onset of the syllable).

   b. Iraqi Arabic speakers insert the same vowel [i] under the same circumstances; however, they insert the [i] before the two consonants rather than between them. This in effect creates an extra syllable consisting of the [i] and the first of the two consonants, which is more in keeping with the syllable structures of Iraqi Arabic.

c. The third form provides the clue. In both the A and B forms of Arabic, the final syllable begins with the consonant cluster [tl] prior to [i] insertion. In Egyptian Arabic this would be broken up by inserting an [i] between the [t] and the [l], whereas in Iraqi Arabic, the [i] would be inserted before the [tl]. From this it can be deduced that A is Iraqi Arabic and B is Egyptian Arabic.

12. *Language development.*

**Part One.** Telegraphic stage.

**Part Two.** Answers may vary here, but consistency is important. Hyphens have been inserted in the sentences below to make clear which morphemes are being counted in this sample answer. Morpheme count:

| | |
|---|---|
| a. Mikey not see him. | [4] |
| b. Where ball go? | [3] |
| c. Look Mommy, doggie. | [3] |
| d. Big doggie. | [2] |
| e. He no bite ya. | [4] |
| f. He eat-s mud. | [4] |
| g. Kitty hid-ing. | [3] |
| h. Grampie wear glasses. | [3] |
| i. He funny. | [2] |
| j. He love-s hamburger-s. | [5] |
| k. Daddy ride bike. | [3] |
| l. That-'s mines. | [3] |
| m. That my toy. | [3] |
| n. Him sleep-ing. | [3] |
| o. Want more milk. | [3] |
| p. Read moon book. | [3] |
| q. Me want that. | [3] |
| r. Teddy up. | [2] |
| s. Daddy 'puter. | [2] |
| t. 'Puter broke. | [2] |
| u. Cookie-s and milk!!! | [4] |
| v. Me Superman. | [2] |
| w. Mommy-'s angry. | [3] |
| x. Allgone kitty. | [2] |
| y. Here my bat-ball. | [4] |

**Part Three.** MLU in morphemes is the total number of morphemes (75) divided by the number of utterances (25) = 3. MLU in words is 66 divided by 25 = 2.64.

**Part Four.** *Allgone* is probably not analyzed as two morphemes (or words), but is a fixed expression, so one morpheme.

*Batball* probably means 'baseball' (ball that you hit with a bat). Since it is a novel word, Sam has put together two words/ morphemes creatively. It must be two morphemes.

*Glasses* is likely one morpheme because it is not semantically plural.

*Cookies* is semantically plural, so it is likely two morphemes.

13. *Telegraphic stage.*

   a. Answers will vary. One hypothesis (hypothesis A) is that children drop subjects because they have limited processing resources, for example, limited memory capacity. Another hypothesis (hypothesis B) might be that children drop subjects for pragmatic reasons, when the identity of the subject is contextually salient, e.g., the subject is the child himself, the speaker. A third possibility (hypothesis C) is that children drop subjects for grammatical reasons; that is, they "assume" that English is a language like Italian that allows subjects to be dropped; they have "misset" the UG parameter that identified English as a language that requires subjects to be overtly expressed and Italian as one that does not (see chapter 4).

   b. A possible objection to hypothesis A is that children drop subjects but not objects. Why would subjects be favored if this were just the effect of an overload in processing? A possible objection to hypothesis B is that the identity of the subject is not always predictable from context; that is, the subject is not always the child himself, as can be seen in the examples. Also, it is hard to define what is contextually salient to the child. A possible objection to hypothesis C is that if the child "missets" her parameter, how does she ever learn the correct setting for English? What information in the input would tell her that the subject is always required in English? She will hear colloquial expressions such as "wanna leave?," which might be misleading. Also, there is a logical problem: just because all (or most) of the sentences she hears have overt subjects, she cannot conclude from this that the next sentence might have a dropped subject. For this, she would need "negative evidence"; that is, explicit information that it is not grammatical to drop subjects in English except in very restricted cases such as "wanna leave." Parents do not often provide children with explicit information about the rules of the language.

14. *Overextensions.*

   a. shape: all items in column B are round.
   b. shape and function: all items in column B are round and edible.
   c. characteristic activity: all items in column B fly.
   d. appearance: all items in column B are furry, four-legged animals.
   e. appearance and size: all items in column B are vehicles larger than a car.
   f. gender: all items in column B are either men or associated with men.
   g. shape: all items in column B are shaped like a moon at some point in its phase: either a full moon (like the chrome dial of the dishwasher), a half-moon (like the lemon slice), a crescent moon (half a Cheerio), or a sliver of a moon (the hangnail).

# Chapter 10

1. *Speech errors.*

   (1) brake fluid → blake fruid
       a. phonological
       b. reversal or exchange of phonologically similar segments (they are both liquids) in consonant clusters

   (2) drink is the curse of the working classes → work is the curse of the drinking classes
       a. lexical
       b. exchange of words

   (3) I have to smoke a cigarette with my coffee → . . . smoke my coffee with a cigarette
       a. syntactic constituent
       b. exchange of NPs "a cigarette" and "my coffee"

   (4) untactful → distactful
       a. morphological
       b. substitution of prefix with similar meaning

   (5) an eating marathon → a meeting arathon
       a. phonological
       b. shift of word-initial consonant from the second to the first word; change of *an* to *a*, in keeping with morphological rules of English

   (6) executive committee → executor committee
       a. morphological
       b. substitution of suffix

   (7) lady with the dachshund → lady with the Volkswagen
       a. semantic
       b. substitution of word with similar semantic features (in this case, "small, German")

   (8) Are we taking a bus back → are we taking the buck bass
       a. phonological segment
       b. exchange of coda consonants /s/ and /k/

   (9) he broke the crystal on my watch → he broke the whistle on my crotch
       a. phonological
       b. exchange of syllable consonant onsets /kr/ and /w/ and deletion of the /t/ present in the intended *crystal*

**110**

(10) a phonological rule → a phonological fool
   a. phonological
   b. substitution due to perseveration of /f/

(11) pitch and stress → piss and stretch
   a. phonological
   b. exchange of final consonants

(12) Lebanon → lemadon
   a. phonological feature
   b. exchange of features "voiced stop" with "nasal" in /b/ and /n/, resulting in /m/ and /d/

(13) speech production → preach seduction
   a. phonological
   b. exchange of syllable onsets (/sp/ and /pr/) with deletion of second occurrence of /p/

(14) he's a New Yorker → he's a New Yorkan
   a. morphological
   b. substitution of derivational suffix with same meaning

(15) I'd forgotten about that → I'd forgot abouten that
   a. morphological
   b. shift of inflectional verb suffix to preposition

(16) It can deliver a large payload → It can deliver a large payroll
   a. lexical
   b. substitution of a phonetically similar word; in the context of a political election during an economically difficult time, "large payrolls" are on everyone's mind, so the slip is probably influenced by the context of the election

(17) He made headlines → He made hairlines
   a. lexical
   b. substitution of a phonetically similar word *hair* for *head*; in the context of a barbershop, *hair* is semantically relevant, as are (potentially receding) *hairlines*.

(18) I never heard of classes on Good Friday → I never heard of classes on April 9
   a. syntactic constituent
   b. substitution of an NP that shares some of the meaning with the intended NP; in the context of a year in which Good Friday fell on April 9, these phrases may have overlapping meanings. However, the ways in which the phrases differ semantically are crucially what make this slip of the tongue funny. Good Friday is not always on April 9, and there is nothing strange about having class on April 9 per se.

2. *Understanding and resolving ambiguity.*

(1) *For those of you who have children and don't know it, we have a nursery downstairs.*

Ambiguity: *It* could refer to having children or to the fact that there is a nursery downstairs.

Likely: *It* refers to the fact that there is a nursery downstairs.

Knowledge: Most people know whether they have children.

(2) *The police were asked to stop drinking in public places.*

Ambiguity: The subject of *drinking* could be the police or other persons.

Likely: Other persons.

Knowledge: The police are usually the enforcers, not the violators.

(3) *Our bikinis are exciting; they are simply the tops.*

Ambiguity: The word *tops* may mean 'excellent' or 'the bra half of a bikini.'

Likely: 'Excellent.'

Knowledge: Bikinis generally consist of a top half and a bottom half.

(4) *It's time we made smoking history.*

Ambiguity: 'We are eliminating smoking' (analogous to *It's time we made smoking illegal*), or 'we are going to do something so important in regards to smoking that it will be written about in history books' (analogous to *It's time we made political history*).

Likely: Both readings are likely.

Knowledge: If some group managed to eliminate smoking, they would be "making smoking history" both in terms of (1) ending smoking and (2) doing something so important in terms of smoking that it'll be written down in the history books.

(5) *Do you know the time?*

Ambiguity: This is a pragmatic ambiguity and may be a literal question about what you know or an indirect request for the time.

Likely: A request for the time.

Knowledge: It is more likely that someone wants to know the time than that someone wants to know whether someone else knows the time. (Note that this apparent question may also be used as indirect criticism to someone who is taking a long time to do something.)

(6) *Concerned with spreading violence, the president called a press conference.*

Ambiguity: The subject of *spreading violence* may be others or may be the president. *Spreading violence* may also be an Adjective-Noun construction and have the meaning 'the spread of violence,' though

**112**

this is indistinguishable from the Verb-Object construction where the subject is some non-specified other group of people.

Likely: Others are spreading the violence.

Knowledge: The president is not likely to spread violence, and even if she were, she would not call a press conference about it.

(7) *The ladies of the church have cast off clothing of every kind and they may be seen in the church basement Friday.*

Ambiguity: *Cast off* is an adjective describing clothing (in which case it would be hyphenated, strictly speaking), or it is a verb meaning 'disrobe,' whose object is *clothing*. Depending on which case, *they* in the second clause may refer to the old clothing or to the lady strippers.

Likely: *Cast off* describes the clothing, and *they* refers to that clothing.

Knowledge: Church ladies usually don't strip, especially in the church.

(8) *She earned little as a whiskey maker but he loved her still.*

Ambiguity: *Still* could be the adverb, meaning continuing to the present time, or *still* could be the noun, the piece of machinery used in distilling whiskey.

Likely: *Still* is the adverb.

Knowledge: Men are more likely to love women than pieces of machinery. In addition, the "but" between the two clauses suggests that the second clause is true despite the first clause. It makes more sense that he loves the woman despite the fact that she doesn't make much money than that he loves the woman's machine despite the fact that the woman doesn't make much money.

(9) *The butcher backed into the meat grinder and got a little behind in his work.*

Ambiguity: There are two ambiguities: i) *the meat grinder* could be the person or the machine, and ii) *behind* could be the noun 'buttocks' or it could mean 'delayed.' In addition to these ambiguities, *backed into* is vague. It means 'move in a backward motion into,' but this could be while in a car or other vehicle or while on foot or crawling, etc. The two most likely meanings of the entire sentences are:

'The butcher backed into the meat grinder (the person) (while in a car) and got a little behind (delayed) in his work.'

'(While standing) the butcher backed into the meat grinder (the machine) and got a little behind (buttocks) in his work.'

Likely: *Meat grinder* most likely means the person and *behind* most likely means 'delayed.'

Knowledge: It is more common that one would have a minor traffic accident by backing into a person, which would delay them, than that one would back up into a machine that might grind some of their buttocks.

113

(10) *A dog gave birth to puppies near the road and was cited for littering.*

Ambiguity: *Litter* refers to trash or a group of newborn puppies. The joke is suggesting an ambiguity between *litter* 'trash' + *ing* = *littering* 'the act of leaving trash where one shouldn't' and *litter* 'a group of newborn puppies' + *ing* = *littering*, which might mean 'the act of having a litter of puppies.'

Likely: The joke is funny because neither is very likely, but for different reasons.

Knowledge: Semantically *littering* meaning the act of having a litter of puppies is more likely, since we know the dog just had puppies, but we know that this word doesn't mean that. And while *littering* is a perfectly good word meaning the act of leaving trash where one shouldn't, it doesn't make sense here because the dog didn't leave trash anywhere; she had puppies.

(11) *A hole was found in the nudist camp wall. The police are looking into it.*

Ambiguity: There are two ambiguities here. *Looking into* can mean 'peering into' or 'investigating.' *It* can be referring to the fact that there is a hole in the wall or to the hole itself. The most likely readings from these two ambiguities are:

'A hole was found in the nudist camp wall and the police are peering into that hole.'

'A hole was found in the nudist camp wall and the police are investigating why there is a hole there.'

Likely: Most likely *looking into* means 'investigating' and *it* refers to the fact that there is a hole.

Knowledge: The police are more likely to investigate a potential crime than to be peeping in on nudists. But the sentence is amusing because the other reading is not impossible.

(12) *A sign on the lawn at a drug rehab center said, "Keep off the Grass."*

Ambiguity: *Grass* could mean 'lawn' or 'marijuana.'

Likely: 'Lawn'

Knowledge: Given that the sign is on the lawn, the more likely reading is that the sign means, 'Keep off the lawn.' But, given that the sign is at a drug rehab center, the other meaning is not impossible, which makes the sentence amusing.

(13) *Red Tape Holds Up New Bridge*

Ambiguity: *Red tape* refers to paperwork or to structural support.

Likely: Paper work.

Knowledge: Tape of any color is not used to build bridges.

114

(14) *Kids Make Nutritious Snacks*

Ambiguity: Kids are making food or are themselves food.

Likely: Kids are making food.

Knowledge: Kids are generally not eaten.

(15) *Sex Education Delayed, Teachers Request Training.*

Ambiguity: Teachers intend to teach sex education or to be taught about sex.

Likely: Teachers intend to teach sex education.

Knowledge: Teachers would not openly request sexual training.

3. *Temporal ambiguities.* Answers will vary. Here are three sample answers:

   i. *Mary believed the boy was lying.* There are several layers of ambiguity here, both of which have to do with perfectivity—i.e., are the past events / states over or do they continue into the present moment? *Mary believed the boy was lying* could that mean she used to believe that but no longer does, or it could mean that she used to believe it and continues to do so. Likewise, *the boy was lying* could mean that he was lying but stopped or that he was lying and continues to lie. There is no way to resolve these ambiguities without more information.

   ii. *I decided to go to the party yesterday.* The ambiguity lies in what *yesterday* applies to—the decision or the going to the party. So this sentence could mean *Yesterday, I decided to go to the party*: the decision to go to the party was made yesterday and it is not specified when the party is—it could be any time after the decision, including yesterday and two weeks from yesterday. The other possibility is that the party occurred yesterday and that the decision to go the party was made at some point in time before the going to the party—including yesterday and two weeks before yesterday. There is no way to resolve these ambiguities without more information.

   iii. *I'm going to buy my tickets for my trip to Mexico next week.* This is similar to the example above: the scope of *next week* is not clear here. Is the buying of the tickets occurring next week, or the trip? Or both? Again, there is no way to resolve this ambiguity without more information, though prosody may give us a clue in this case.

4. *Headlines.*

   a. The principle of late closure explains the funny interpretation of these headlines: *to people* is interpreted as belonging to *what they are doing to people* and *in checkout line* is interpreted as belonging to *after 18 years in checkout line.*

   b. Moving the misinterpreted phrases elsewhere in the headlines gets rid of the unintended meanings:

   *Physicists Thrilled to Explain [to People] What They Are Doing*

   *Two Sisters Reunited [in Checkout Line] After 18 Years*

   c. Answers will vary.

5. *Garden Path Sentences.* The principle of minimal attachment can explain the asymmetry in the processing of these sentences.

   (1)   *the message* is easily interpretable as the object of the verb *understood*, while *the snow* isn't.

   (2)   *the mistake* is easily interpretable as the object of the verb *admitted*, while *the airplane* isn't.

   (3)   *the large wolf* is easily interpretable as the object of the verb *feared* while *the dress* isn't.

6. *Priming.*

   (1)   Answers will vary, but most people will probably "fall for it". Priming is effective here for two reasons: (1) *yolk* is being primed with members of its phonological lexical neighborhood, and (2) most people don't know what the white of an egg is called; even if they do, *yolk* is a much more common word than *albumin*.

   (2)   Answers will vary, but many people will likely not point out that survivors are not buried. Here the priming is not phonological but rather semantic: in the scenario of an airplane crash, all things semantically related to an airplane crash may be primed, including *survivors*. Even if you have been explicitly told that there are no survivors, this does not prevent the priming of this word. The priming of *survivors* facilitates the processing error that many will experience. If you asked them instead ". . . where will you bury the monkeys?", a much higher percentage would most likely object and ask, "What monkeys?" as *monkey* is not semantically primed by the scenario of an airplane crash.

7. *The mind and lateralization.* Answers will vary. A student's essay might include some of the following:

   Possible arguments for Sperry's position:
   - Studies on split-brain patients demonstrate differentiation of functions of the right and the left hemispheres.
   - Damage to the right hemisphere may result in nonlinguistic cognitive deficits, with language remaining largely intact. And conversely, left hemisphere damage frequently results in aphasia without necessarily affecting other cognitive functions. This argues for separate minds with separate functions.

   Possible arguments for Eccles's position:
   - Eccles must believe that thought cannot be expressed without language. If this is so, since only the left hemisphere is specialized for language, it can be argued that the right hemisphere cannot think.
   - The left hemisphere is specialized not only for language but also for mathematical and some other cognitive abilities, which are purely human.

There is, however, growing evidence that the physical brain and the mind that results from its neural architecture and functions is highly complex on both sides, that distinct cognitive systems are represented and processed in different locations, and that these interact in mental behavior. Furthermore, thinking does not require language, as shown by split-brain patients and by humans who never acquire language but who are functionally capable in other cognitive spheres. Deaf individuals, for example, who have not been exposed to sign language are still capable of learning and thinking.

8. *How words are stored in the brain.*

   a. The substituted words in group (i) are in the same syntactic category as the stimulus words and are semantically related. They are not phonologically similar. In group (ii), the substituted words are, for the most part, derivationally related to the stimulus words, which are verbs. In the case where the substituted word is not directly derived from the stimulus word (speak/discussion), it is still semantically related to it.

   b. The words in these two groups show that words are connected to each other according to semantic class and syntactic category.

9. *Aphasic language.* Answers will vary.

   a. *There is under a horse a new sidesaddle.*

      In nonaphasic language, the prepositional phrase *(under a horse)* follows the noun phrase *(a new sidesaddle)* in sentences of this form. Also, in normal speech, the preposition would be *on* rather than *under*. It is also likely that the article should be *the*, not *a*. If *horse* is not definite, the usual expression would be *there is a new sidesaddle on one of the horses.*

   b. *In girls we see many happy days.*

      This sentence is grammatically well formed but it is not easily interpreted.

      Metaphorical speech and aphasic speech share some common ground.

   c. *I'll challenge a new bike.*

      In nonaphasic language, the verb *challenge* generally, but not always, takes a human or abstract noun (e.g., *challenge the judge/law*). Here, the verb is followed by an inanimate, concrete object, which is unusual. The intended meaning is unclear without further context.

   d. *I surprise no new glamour.*

      The verb *surprise* must take an animate object (e.g., *surprise a friend*). Here, the verb is followed by an inanimate, abstract object. The intended meaning is unclear and the sentence is uninterpretable.

   e. *Is there three chairs in this room?*

      The verb *is*—the singular form of the verb *be*—should be in the plural form *are* to agree in number with the subject of the sentence (*three chairs*).

f. *Mike and Peter is happy.*

The verb should agree with the number of the subject noun phrase, which, in this case, is plural (*Mike and Peter*), and should therefore be *are*.

g. *Bill and John likes hot dogs.*

Same as item f. The verb *likes* is singular but the subject is plural.

h. *Proliferate is a complete time about a word that is correct.*

In nonaphasic language, *proliferate* is a verb and cannot be used as the subject of a sentence. The sentence is uninterpretable.

i. *Went came in better than it did before.*

In nonaphasic language, a past tense verb form such as *went* cannot be used as the subject of a sentence. It is not clear what the intended meaning of the sentence is.

10. *Brain damage and neural basis of language.* It is possible to investigate different functions of a complex automobile engine by systematically damaging individual parts to see what the effect might be. This is also true of brain research; lesions in different parts of the brain result in specific linguistic or other cognitive deficits. Syntax can be impaired with semantics and phonology retained, and vice versa. Engines are like brains in that they can limp along without all cylinders firing, with an impeded fuel flow, with short circuits, with computer components such as oxygen sensors failing, etc.

Individual answers to the question will vary. If the question is assigned by instructors, students should be encouraged to consult the literature to show the kinds of deficits that can occur due to damage to different lesion sites.

11. *Evidence for lateralization.* Sample answers:
    - Brain damage research provides strong evidence for lateralization of brain functions. Right and left hemispheric damage affect functioning of different cognitive systems.
    - Studies of childhood brain lesions suggest that the human brain is lateralized to the left for language from birth.
    - Research on individuals with split brains offers further evidence for language lateralization.
    - Results of dichotic listening research support lateralization of brain functions.
    - MRI and PET studies demonstrate that the two hemispheres perform different cognitive functions.

12. *Discussion of Wigan's comment.* Answers will vary. The answers may include discussions of the different cognitive functions that the two hemispheres perform.

13. *Dichotic listening.* Some possible visual stimuli for dichotic listening experiments:
    - Printed words to read. (We would expect to get fewer errors when reporting stimuli presented in the right visual field.)
    - Pictures of objects to copy. (Fewer errors for the stimuli in the left field expected.)
    - Pictures of faces expressing different emotional states, e.g., happy/sad faces, etc. Subjects to say what the emotion is. (Fewer errors in the left field expected.)
    - Printed strings of letters, some of which are words, and some nonwords. Subjects' task is to say whether the string is a word. (Fewer errors in the right visual field.)

14. *Utterances of Broca's and Wernicke's aphasics.*

    a. W

    b. B

    c. W

    d. B

15. *Hamlet.* Possible arguments that Hamlet was a Wernicke's aphasic:
    - His speech here makes little sense.
    - He uses some very odd expressions, such as ". . . eyes purging thick amber and plum-tree gum."

    Possible arguments against this position:
    - There are no neologisms.
    - Although very difficult to interpret, his sentences are almost entirely grammatical.

16. *Research projects.*

    a. *Perfect pitch.* Answers will vary. A student's answer should include a definition of "perfect pitch" and an explanation of how this relates to the critical-age hypothesis. An answer might include some of the following:

    *Definition of perfect pitch*
    - The ability to recognize the pitch of a musical tone without an external reference pitch.

    *Relation to critical-age hypothesis*
    - As with language, the ability to distinguish perfect pitch needs to be exercised at a young age or it will atrophy by adulthood.
    - The critical-age hypothesis states that the ability to learn a grammar develops within a fixed period, from birth to middle childhood, as long as there is linguistic input. Children who are denied linguistic input never master the grammar with native proficiency. The same is true of perfect pitch. If a child has limited exposure to musical input, she will be less likely to develop perfect pitch.

b. *Brain Imaging Technologies*. Answers will vary. The sample answer below is based on information found at www.radiologyinfo.org, www.mayfieldclinic.com and www.nmr.mgh.harvard.edu/martinos/research/technologiesMEG.php. A student's answer should consider several of the methodologies listed below, comparing and contrasting their upsides and downsides freely:

- CT (computer tomography) scan

  Upsides: painless, noninvasive, and accurate; provides very detailed images; fast and simple; cost-effective; less sensitive to patient movement than MRI; provides real-time imaging; no radiation remains in a patient's body after a CT examination; x-rays used in CT scans usually have no side effects

  Downsides: a slight chance of cancer from excessive exposure to radiation; serious allergic reaction to contrast materials is extremely rare; CT scans are not recommended for pregnant women or children because of the exposure to radiation; nursing mothers should wait 24 hours before resuming breast-feeding

- PET (positron emission tomography) scan

  Upsides: the information provided is unique and often unattainable using other imaging procedures; cost effective and precise; identifies changes in the body at the cellular level

  Downsides: low radiation exposure, but no known long-term adverse effects from such low-dose exposure; allergic reactions to radiopharmaceuticals are extremely rare and are usually mild; injection of the radiotracer may cause slight pain and redness

- MRI (magnetic resonance imaging) scan

  Upsides: noninvasive, with no exposure to ionizing radiation; allergic reaction to contrast material less likely than that used for CT; almost no risk when appropriate safety guidelines are followed

  Downsides: if sedation is used, there are risks of excessive sedation; implanted medical devices that contain metal may malfunction due to the strong magnetic field; nephrogenic systemic fibrosis, which is a rare complication believed to be caused by the injection of high doses of MRI contrast material in patients with very poor kidney function

- fMRI (functional MRI) scan

  Upsides: noninvasive; no exposure to ionizing radiation; can assess both structure and function of brain; almost no risk to the average patient when appropriate safety guidelines are followed

  Downsides: if sedation is used, there are risks of excessive sedation; implanted medical devices that contain metal may malfunction due to the strong magnetic field; nephrogenic systemic fibrosis, which is a rare complication, may be caused by the injection of high doses of MRI contrast material in patients with very poor kidney function

**120**

- SPECT (Single Photon Emission CT) scans

  Upsides: can view blood flow through arteries and veins in the brain; different from either MRI or CT scanning because it can detect reduced blood flow to certain sites

  Downsides: small risk from exposure to radiation, which is less than received during a chest X-ray or CT scan; not safe for women who are pregnant or nursing

- MEG (magnetoencephalography)

  Upsides: completely noninvasive and non-hazardous; localizes and characterizes the electrical activity of the central nervous system by measuring the associated magnetic fields emanating from the brain; the data can be collected in a seated position, allowing more life-like experiments than fMRI; the measurement environment is completely silent, which allows for auditory studies; electrodes do not need to be pasted to the scalp as with EEG

  Downsides: the localization of sources of electrical activity within the brain from magnetic measurement outside the head is complicated; it is difficult to provide reliable information about subcortical sources of brain activity; does not provide structural/anatomical information; the measurements have to be taken in a magnetically shielded room

c. *Reading aloud and reading silently.* Answers will vary. A sample answer follows: Petersen, Fox, Posner, Minton, and Raichle conclude in their article "Positron emission tomographic studies of the cortical anatomy of single-word processing" in *Nature* (Vol. 331, No. 6157, pp. 585–589, 18 February 1988) that different areas of the brain are involved in reading out loud (passive auditory presentation) and reading silently (visual presentation). "For the visual modality, the main cortical activations are in the striate cortex and in a small set of prestriate areas reaching as far anterior as the temporal-occipital boundary" (p. 586) and "for auditory processing, areas of activity were found bilaterally in primary auditory cortex, and left-lateralized in temporoparietal cortex, anterior superior temporal cortex, and inferior anterior cingulate cortex" (p. 587).

17. *Article review project.* Answers will vary. Students' answers should include:

- *Summary of the article.* In this article, the authors argue that understanding the faculty of language involves cooperation among researchers in linguistics, evolutionary biology, anthropology, psychology, and neuroscience. They argue that the faculty of language can be considered in two ways: in a broad sense (including a sensory-motor system, a conceptual-intentional system, and recursion) and in a narrow sense (recursion only). They hypothesize that the mechanism of recursion is the only uniquely human concept of language.

- *Critically review.* Encourage students to be creative and incorporate their knowledge of linguistics and other disciplines (psychology, biology, anthropology, etc.)

18. *Agrammatic aphasics.*

    a. can (be able to), *but, not, be, may, or, will* (future), *might* (possibility)
    b. Evidence comes from the behavior of: (1) aphasics, (2) SLI patients, and (3) late language learners. Students' answers should include specific examples either from the text or from their own research.

19. *Traditional Chinese orthography vs. pinyin.* The location of neural activity is different when Chinese speakers read in these two systems. Evidence for this statement comes from Japanese, which also has two writing systems, *kana* and *kanji.* Japanese speakers with left-hemisphere damage are impaired in their ability to read *kana,* while people with right-hemisphere damage are impaired in their ability to read *kanji.* Also, experiments with normal Japanese speakers show that the right hemisphere is better and faster than the left hemisphere at reading *kanji,* while the left hemisphere is better and faster than the right at reading *kana.*

20. *Commenting on Thatcher's quote.* Answers will vary. Students can take either side, as this issue is controversial. A sample answer could include some of the following:
    There are gender differences in the brain having to do with how men and women process and use language.
    - Men are more likely to become aphasics with left-hemisphere damage.
    - Males outnumber females about 3 to 4 times for stuttering and 10 times for severe dyslexia.
    - Males are diagnosed with autism, including language impairment, at a rate of 3 to 4 times higher than females.

    There are no gender differences in the brain having to do with how men and women process and use language.
    - fMRI studies have shown that men and women have similar brain activity (that is, both genders exhibit a strong left lateralization) in both phonological and semantic tasks.
    - Frequent and large-population studies fail to indicate gender differences in verbal ability.

21. *Emergence.* Answers will vary. The information for the following sample answer was taken from Wikipedia (http://en.wikipedia.org/wiki /Emergence):

    Jeffrey Goldstein defines emergence as 'the arising of novel and coherent structures, patterns and properties during the process of self-organization in complex systems' (Corning, 2002. "The Re-Emergence of "Emergence": A Venerable Concept of Search of a Theory", *Complexity* 7(6): 18–30).

This concept, though not this term, has been around since the time of Aristotle. Some believe there are types of emergence phenomena within linguistics, including language change (Keller, 1994. *On Language Change: The Invisible Hand in Language*, Routledge) and sociolinguistic conventions (Määttä, 2000. "Mistä on pienet säännöt tehty?", *Virittäjä* 2: 203–221).

Even though they don't use the term "emergence," this idea can be seen in Chomsky's phrasing "a certain level of complexity" and Gould's phrasing "perhaps the brain grew in size and became capable of all kinds of things which were not part of the original properties." The theory of emergence seems very compatible with the types of ideas expressed here. However, Pinker's quote about "precise wiring" seems different from the first two, in that it doesn't reference the idea of emergence, and perhaps is incompatible with it.

# Chapter 11

1. *Voiceprints*. The following are some speech signals that can differ by speaker:

   **Pitch:** Some voices are higher than others. Male voices tend to be lower in pitch, but even within the same sex, pitch differences occur. These differences are due to physical differences in the larynx, vocal cords, and vocal tract.

   **Nasality:** Some voices seem to be more nasal than others, even when not producing nasal sounds. These differences are due to physical differences in the nasal cavity and velum.

   **Timbre or voice quality:** Some voices are described as having a clear or bell-like quality, while others seem to have a rasping or creaky quality. This is due to physical differences in the larynx and oral/nasal cavities.

   **Intonational patterns:** Some voices tend to be more monotone than others; that is, there are fewer differences between high and low pitch. This is due to individual speech habits.

   **Tempo or speed:** Some individuals speak more rapidly than others. This is due to individual speech habits. Also, the content and context of the speech affects speech rate.

   **Unstressed vowel deletion:** Some speakers delete or slur over unstressed syllables. This may be due to speech rate or individual speech habits.

   **Dialect differences** also show up in spectrograms. These could be used to help identify a given speaker for as many reasons as there are dialect differences.

2. *Translation*. Sample answers are given below using German as the target language. The first line under the English sentence is a word-for-word translation from a bilingual dictionary.

   The next line, in italics, is the grammatically correct translation. The last line is a word-for-word translation back into English.

   (1) The    children    will      eat      the    fish.
   Das   Kinder    werden   essen    das    Fisch.
   *Die Kinder werden den Fisch essen.*
   The children will the fish eat.

(2) Send       the    professor   a      letter   from  your  new  school.
Schicken das    Professor  ein   Brief   von   Ihr  neu  Schule.
*Schicken Sie dem Professor einen Brief aus Ihrer neuen Schule.*
Send you the professor a letter from your new school.

(3) The   fish   will    be     eaten   by    the   children.
Das   Fisch  werden  sein  essen   von  das  Kinder.
*Der Fisch wird von den Kindern gegessen werden.*
The fish will by the children eaten be.

(4) Who  is    the   person  that  is    hugging  that  dog?
Wer  sein  das   Mensch  das  sein  umarmen  das   Hund?
*Wer ist der Mensch, der den Hund umarmt?*
Who is the person that the dog hug?

(5) The   spirit  is    willing,  but   the   flesh   is    weak.
Das   Geist  sein  willig   aber  das   Fleisch  sein  schwach.
*Der Geist ist willig, aber das Fleisch ist schwach.*
The spirit is willing but the flesh is weak.

a. Difficulties involved in translation:

  i. German has several different forms for the determiner *the*. The one
     you use depends on the gender, number, and case of the accompany-
     ing noun. In this exercise, you are forced to pick one at random (we
     used *das* throughout).

  ii. In this task, you are forced to use the form of the verb that is found
      in the dictionary (the infinitive), even if you know that German has
      subject-verb agreement on the verb as well as tensed forms.

  iii. There are many different German words that can be translated by
       the English word *by*; there is no way to know which of them is the
       correct one (if any).

  iv. The English word *is* is not found in the dictionary because it is an
      inflected form and the dictionary has only infinitive verb forms. To
      find the corresponding word, you have to know the infinitive of *is*
      (*be*) and look up the German word for it.

  v. Even if idiomatic expressions such as *The spirit is willing, but the
     flesh is weak* could be translated into grammatical sentences, there
     is no guarantee and little chance that the result will be idiomatic in
     the target language.

  vi. In German subordinate clauses, verbs occur in final position, but in
      English, verbs follow subjects. A translation of a sentence like (4),
      which has a relative clause, cannot reflect the proper word order in
      German unless the ordering of words is changed.

b. A word-for-word translation from German to English would encoun-
   ter the same problems with word forms and word order. Even a knowl-
   edgeable translator will have the same difficulty with word meanings

mentioned in (a). For example, the German translation of (5) might translate back to English as 'The ghost is ready but the meat is weak.'

3. *Text processing.* A computer can be used to measure various statistical properties of the known works of Marlowe and Shakespeare. The properties have to do with lexical usage, sentence length, sentence type (percentage of passives, for example), and many other features. The computer would assign to each author a profile of his or her work based on the analysis. An unknown work could be similarly analyzed and compared to each author's profile. The closer match would suggest the author of the unknown work.

4. *Speech synthesis.* The following are just a few of the many possible answers:

   i. Announcements of routine items on the radio such as weather reports. A computer could be programmed to interpret the raw data of weather—temperature, sky covering, wind direction and speed, etc.—and produce a natural language report that would be pronounced by the speech synthesizer.

   ii. Everyday communication by people who are unable to talk because of an injury or defect.

   iii. Programmable talking toys or games (dolls or robots, for example).

   iv. Teaching correct pronunciation of words and sentences in a foreign language.

   v. Telephone applications—e.g., information, weather reports, arrival and departure times of airplanes and trains, etc.

   vi. Automated bank tellers: for example, usage instructions and results of transactions.

   vii. Announcements of arrival and departure times of aircraft and trains in airports and railroad stations.

   viii. Notifications that something is "ready for pickup," such as pills at the pharmacy.

   ix. Election campaigning.

5. *Speech recognition.* The following are just a few of the many possible answers:

   i. Automated polling by telephone. The answers from the people polled would be recognized by the computer.

   ii. Teaching of foreign languages by computer. Answers in the foreign language would be recognized by the computer, which could make pronunciation suggestions.

   iii. Transactions with the telephone company. The telephone company computer would recognize such expressions as *call collect,* etc. (As of this writing, such systems have been implemented.)

iv. Speech recognizers could be used to recognize distorted speech caused by disease, injury, deafness, etc., and produce a written or synthesized "translation."

v. Catalog ordering by phone.

vi. Navigation through a complex automated answering system such as might be found in the department of transportation in state government.

6. *ELIZA.*

   a. Answers may vary. For example, if you say, "When I came here I was tired," ELIZA answers, "Why do you tell me you were tired just now?" This is intelligent because it is meaningful and syntactically correct; the sentence features correct pronouns; the past tense is correctly recognized; and the use of "just now" suggests the timeliness of the action.

   b. Answers may vary. For example, if you ask ELIZA, "Why do pigs have wings?" or "Do pigs have wings?" or "Should pigs have wings?," you get the same non-answer, namely "Please go on." Whenever you answer "yes" to a question from ELIZA, she asks, "Are you sure?"

   c. Answers may vary. For example, ELIZA will copy a relative clause or a verb phrase in its answer, so if you tell ELIZA, "My brother who is the youngest is leaving home," ELIZA will respond, "Who else who is the youngest is leaving home?"

7. *Torment the computer.* Sample answers: (1) relegate = re + leg + ate; (2) seed = see + d; (3) pensive = pen + s + ive; (4) expensive = ex + pensive or ex + pen + s + ive; (5) sheer = she + er

8. *Pronouncing names.* Answers will vary. With the multicultural Los Angeles phonebook, we averaged less than two!

9. *A Space Odyssey.* Answers will vary. HAL demonstrates native ability in all levels of grammar: phonetics, phonology, morphology, syntax, and semantics. In addition, he has a profound understanding of language use in context. Answers should include a number of specific examples to illustrate HAL's knowledge. For example, when HAL says "I think you know what the problem is just as well as I do," he demonstrates knowledge of complex sentence structure, the semantics of "just" and "as well as," and a pragmatic awareness of what "the problem" refers to.

10. *British National Corpus.* Answers will vary. Below are sample answers for 10 words we looked up.

    i. *coronals*: no instance of *coronals* was found in the corpus. This isn't surprising, as it is a very technical phonetic term. A search for *coronal* retrieved 34 tokens. None of these instances exhibited the use of *coronal* in the linguistic sense. The majority of these were used in medical or astrophysical contexts.

ii. *diphthong*: 39 tokens of *diphthong* were found in the corpus. Most instances seemed to have the linguistic, phonetic sense of the word as in the glossary.

iii. *larynx*: 91 instances were found. The 50 sample tokens provided all seemed to have the meaning of *larynx* found in the glossary.

iv. *phonology*: 175 instances were found. The tokens in the 50 sample sentences displayed all had the sense as in the glossary.

v. *sisters*: 1960 tokens were found. Of the 50 sample sentences returned, none had the sense in the glossary. Most had the genealogical sense of female sibling.

vi. *slang*: 206 tokens were found. Most of the 50 sample sentences showed the meaning in the glossary. But some didn't. For example, linguists would probably use *jargon* instead of *slang* to describe "hook" in the following example from the corpus: "the word 'hook' is Hollywood slang for the distinctive twist in the plot set-up of an otherwise familiar generic story" (from: London: *The Daily Telegraph* plc, 1992).

vii. *suffix*: 151 instances were found. Most of the sample results showed the use of *suffix* as described in the glossary. However, one instance stood out that showed a different meaning: "Everyday conversation became a minefield, peppered by sentences booby trapped by Wayne's trademark deflationary suffix, 'Not!'" (from *The Face*. London: Nick Logan, 1992). Since Wayne's "Not!" is not affixed at the end of a morpheme or stem, a linguist would not call this a suffix. The writer here seems to use the term suffix because of the fact that "Not!" in this sense occurs at the *end* of the entire sentence, thus perhaps metaphorically "suffixed" to the sentence.

viii. *trill*: 44 instances were found. The two main meanings represented were (i) the linguistic sense as defined in the glossary and meanings metaphorically related to this and (ii) the musical sense and other meanings metaphorically related to this.

ix. *unbound*: 47 instances were found. None of them had the linguistic sense as in the glossary.

x. *vowel*: 401 instances were found. Of the 50 randomly displayed, all had the same meaning as in the glossary. This is unsurprising, as it is hard to imagine what else *vowel* might mean.

11. *Culturomics.* Answers will vary. "Pros" of including obsolete English words as belonging to English may include that these words are obsolete *English* words, not—for example—obsolete French words or obsolete Russian words. Furthermore, the fact that a word is not currently in use does not necessarily prevent it from being used again in the future. On the "con" side, students may mention that including words that are no longer in use is a slippery slope. If we count obsolete English words as belonging to the English vocabulary, then why not "obsolete" proto-Germanic words? or

proto-Indo-European words? Where is the cut-off? One obvious cut-off would be to say that we could words as belonging to modern English only if they are currently in use.

12. *Research exercise.* Answers will vary.

13. *Research exercise.* Answers will vary.

# Chapter 12

1. *Pictograms.*

   **Part One.**   The following are sample answers:

   a.  eye:

   b.  a boy:

   c.  two boys:

   d.  library:

   e.  tree:

   f.  forest:

   g.  war:

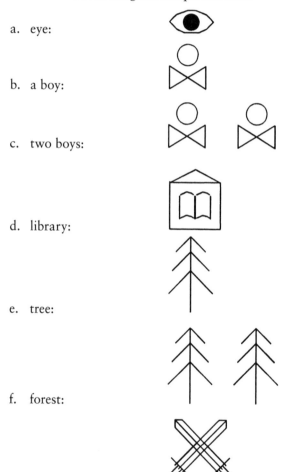

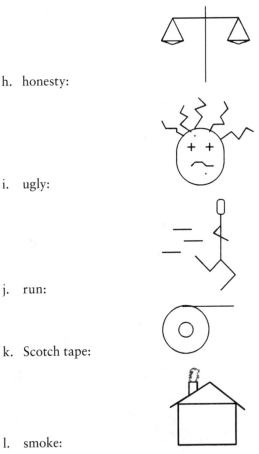

h. honesty:

i. ugly:

j. run:

k. Scotch tape:

l. smoke:

**Part Two.** The most difficult words to symbolize are words like *honesty* and *ugly*. *Honesty* is an abstract word without a physical referent. The picture drawn above is not a good one, since it symbolizes equality or justice but not really honesty. *Ugly* is difficult to picture because the concept is subjective in that what is ugly to one person or culture may not be so to another. It is also difficult to represent the difference between expressions that refer to an exact number of things (like two boys) and words that refer to a large group of things (like *forest*). In addition, it is difficult to distinguish between verbs (like *run*), noun phrases (*running man*), and sentences (*a man runs*).

**Part Three.** Words whose meanings are abstract concepts such as *internalized, unconscious, competence,* etc., are difficult to portray. This is also true of grammatical morphemes such as *of* and *the, is* versus *was, that* or *which,* etc.

2. *Rebuses.*

   **Part One.** Sample answers are given below.

a. tearing (tear + ring)

b. icicle (eye + sickle)

c. bareback (bear + back)

d. cookies (cook + keys)

**Part Two.** Such a system would create problems in attempting to represent, for example, synonyms such as *chair* and *seat.* In addition, as stated above, not all English words can be easily represented in this way. For example, the word *tragedy* is hard to represent as a combination of pictures; how would one symbolize the syllables *tra, ged, y?* It would also be

**132**

difficult or impossible to maintain consistency so that the same set of pictures always gives the same message. Variation in pronunciation could have a disastrous effect in an attempt to understand the pictures.

3. *Non-Roman alphabetic letters.* Sample answers:

A. Alphabetic letters:

| | |
|---|---|
| t | ! |
| r | @ |
| s | # |
| k | $ |
| w | % |
| tʃ | & |
| i | * |
| æ | ? |
| f | + |
| n | = |

B. We have used regular alphabetic spelling (not phonetic spelling) for sounds not specified in the new orthography.

| | | |
|---|---|---|
| a. | character | $?@a$!e@ |
| b. | guest | ge#! |
| c. | cough | $a+ |
| d. | photo | +o!o |
| e. | cheat | &*! |
| f. | rang | @?=g |
| g. | psychotic | #y$o!i$ |
| h. | tree | !@* |

4. *Syllabic systems.*

Syllabary:
A = child [tʃaɪld]
B = ish [ɪʃ]
C = ness [nəs]
D = like [laɪk]
E = je [dʒɛ]
F = su (from *Jesuit*) or zoo [zu]
G = wit [wɪt]
H = life [laɪf]
I = less or lous [ləs]
J = le (from *lethal*) or ly [li]
K = thal [θəl]
L = le (from *lesson*) [lɛ]
M = son [sən]

**133**

Syllabic representations:

a. child-ish-ness:    ABC
b. child-like:        AD
c. Je-su-it:          EFG
d. life-less-ness:    HIC
e. like-ly:           DJ
f. zoo:               F
g. wit-ness:          GC
h. le-thal:           JK
i. jea-lous:          EI
j. wit-less:          GI
k. les-son:           LM

5. *Pronunciation and spelling.*

|     | A       | B           | Reason |
|-----|---------|-------------|--------|
| a.  | I am    | iamb        | The orthographic *b* in *iamb* reveals its morphological relationship with *iambic*, in which the *b* is pronounced. In addition, English phonological rules will predictably delete the /b/ in *iamb*. |
| b.  | goose   | produce     | Although the *c* in *produce* is pronounced /s/, in *production*, it is pronounced [k]. It is helpful to have morphemes that occur in different contexts spelled the same. |
| c.  | fashion | complication | The *t* is pronounced [t] in *complicate,* a morpheme that occurs in *complication.* The spelling reveals this. |
| d.  | Newton  | organ       | The *a* is pronounced [æ] in *organic*; the *o* is pronounced [o] in *Newtonian*. All vowels reduce to [ə] in unstressed positions. Spelling them differently reflects their pronunciations under stress. |
| e.  | no      | know        | The *k* is pronounced in words like *acknowledge.* Spelling *know* with a *k* reveals what the morpheme is and what it means. |
| f.  | hymn    | him         | The *n* is pronounced in *hymnal,* and should thus be spelled the same wherever the morpheme occurs. English phonology predicts that the final *n* after an *m* will be deleted, that is, not pronounced. |

6. *Pronunciation and spelling.*

| | A | B | Reason |
|---|---|---|---|
| a. | mingle | long | The *g* is pronounced in *longer*, showing the relation between *long* and *longer*. |
| b. | line | children | The morpheme *child* occurs in *children*, and the spelling reveals this. In addition, there is a regular correspondence between [aɪ] and [ɪ] in other words in English: compare *line—linear, sign—signature*. |
| c. | sonar | resound | Both words derive from the morpheme *sound*. Although the *s* in *sound* is voiceless, and the *s* in *resound* is voiced: spelling them both with an *s* shows this relationship. |
| d. | cent | mystic | The *c* in *mystic* is pronounced [s] in *mysticism,* so we retain consistency in the spelling of the morpheme. |
| e. | crumble | bomb | The *b* is pronounced in *bombard*; the spelling of *bomb* with a *b* therefore shows that the multimorphemic word *bombard* includes this root morpheme. In addition, the deletion of the *b* in *bomb* is predictable by phonological rules in English, which delete a final /b/ after a consonant. |
| f. | cats | dogs | In both words, the *s* represents the plural morpheme; the allomorphs /s/, /z/, and /əz/ are predictable by rule. |
| g. | stagnant | design | The *g* is pronounced in *designate*; the spelling relates the two words. The fact that the *g* is not pronounced in *design* (or *sign, malign,* etc.) is predictable by English phonological rules. |
| h. | serene | obscenity | There is a regular correspondence between [i] and [ɛ] in words like *serene/serenity* and *obscene/obscenity*. The different pronunciations of these morphemes are thus predictable by rule; the orthography reflects this, and relates the words with the same morphemes. |

7. *Disambiguation through intonation.*

a. What are we having for dinner, Mother?

If Mother is being asked a question, the intonation on *dinner* is rising and the intonation on *Mother* is falling. If the question is whether

**135**

we are having Mother for dinner, there is a pause between *dinner* and *Mother*; the intonation on *dinner* is rising, and the intonation on *Mother* is rising starting from a higher point.

b. She's a German language teacher.

If the statement is about a language teacher who is German, the main stress is on *German*. If the statement is about someone who is a teacher of the German language, the main stress is on *language*.

c. They formed a student grievance committee.

If the reference is to a committee concerned with student grievances, the main stress would fall on *committee*. The main stress would fall on *grievance* if the reference was to a student committee concerned with grievances.

d. Charles kissed his wife and George kissed his wife too.

If both Charles and George kissed the same person, Charles's wife, stress is on *too*. If each man kissed his own wife, contrastive stress is necessary on the second instance of *his*.

8. *Disambiguation through writing.*

a. They're my brothers' keepers.

The *-s* (/z/) possessive morpheme is not pronounced after a plural noun; thus, singular and plural possessive of *brother* are pronounced identically. In written language, the apostrophe is written after the plural *-s* to indicate the plural possessive, and before the possessive *-s* to indicate the singular possessive.

b. He said, "He will take the garbage out."

In spoken language, this can be either a direct quote, in which case the two pronouns refer to two different people; or an indirect quote, in which case the two pronouns may or may not refer to the same person. In written language, direct quotes are set off by quotation marks, while indirect quotes are not.

c. The red book was read.

This sentence is ambiguous when spoken because the adjective *red* and the passive participle *read* are pronounced the same. Since they are spelled differently, the written form is unambiguous.

d. The flower was on the table.

As in (c), the different spellings of *flower* and *flour* disambiguate the sentence, which in speech could refer to either a plant or flour out of which bread is made.

9. *Identifying writing.*

| | | |
|---|---|---|
| a. | Cherokee | 7 |
| b. | Chinese | 6 |
| c. | German (Gothic style) | 9 |
| d. | Greek | 2 |

| e. | Hebrew | 4 |
| f. | Icelandic | 8 |
| g. | Japanese | 1 |
| h. | Korean | 10 |
| i. | Russian | 3 |
| j. | Twi | 5 |

10. *Identifying languages.*

1. Spanish
2. English
3. French
4. German
5. Italian
6. Portuguese
7. Japanese
8. Russian
9. Polish
10. Serbo-Croatian
11. Greek
12. Turkish
13. Arabic

11. *Comments on Diderot and D'Alembert's quote.* Answers will vary. The essay should include the fact that alphabetical writing systems can be used for any language, independently of the number of sounds the language has. It is not true that Chinese, or any human language, has an "extremely limited number of sounds." Finally, it may be noted that there is an alphabetic writing system for transliterating Chinese ideograms into the Roman alphabet, officially adopted by the People's Republic of China in 1979.

12. *Emoticons.* Answers will vary. Some possible answers were provided in a footnote to the question.

13. *Multiple emoticons, multiple meanings.* Answers will vary. Sample answers:

A. The following emoticons all symbolize smiling:

:-)

(:-)

(^-^)

The following are all used to mean 'I'm sad':

:-(

:^(

:=(

B. $-) can mean 'won the lottery' or 'yuppie.'
    (-: can mean 'left handed' or 'Australian.'
    3:-) can mean 'cow,' 'Bart Simpson,' or 'has curly hair.'
    :-D can express laughter or surprise.
    :-$ can mean 'my lips are wired shut' or can express cynicism.
    :/{ can mean 'not funny' or 'undecided.'

14. *Inventing emoticons.* Answers will vary. Here are some sample answers:
    :* 'love, affection'
    :? 'miscellaneous'
    :{ } 'aaarrggh'
    [8-} 'bug-eyed over that'
    ([:<E 'why grandma, what big teeth you have!'

15. *Punctuating sentences.*
    That, that is, is; that, that is not, is not. That, that is not, is not that, that is; that, that is, is not that, that is not.

16. *Exceptions to "majority rules" in sound-spelling correspondences.* Answers will vary. Sample answers:
    1. The *ei* spelling in *neighbor, sleigh, rein, feign, lei,* and *weigh* is pronounced [e], with exceptions such as *height, feisty,* and *kaleidoscope,* where the *ei* is pronounced as [aɪ].
    2. The *t* spelling in *act, strict,* and *pat* are produced as [t], with exceptions such as *nation, exemption,* and *declaration,* where the *t* is pronounced as [ʃ].
    3. The *th* spelling is pronounced as [θ] as in *thump, thimble,* and *thin,* with exceptions such as *Thomas, sweetheart,* and *sweathouse,* where the *th* is pronounced as [t] or [tʰ].

17. *Nushu.*
    a. Nushu is an ancient logographic writing system.
    b. Nushu, which literally means 'women's writing,' is a writing system created and used exclusively by women in China.
    c. Nushu was created in China.
    d. Nushu was developed in the 15th century. Today, only a handful of women can read and write Nushu.
    e. In feudal China, women were denied a formal education of any kind, so women developed Nushu in secret as a way to read and write.
    f. Answers will vary. Sample answer: In the United States, slaves were denied an education. Thus, slaves could have developed their own writing system.

18. *German spelling reform of 1996.* Answers will vary.

    a. Germany, Austria, Liechtenstein, and Switzerland were involved in the German spelling reform of 1996.

    b. One of the spelling changes seems to offer more orthographic morphological regularity. For example, the word *Schiff + fahrt* used to be spelled *Schiffahrt*, with only two *f*s, and is now spelled *Schifffahrt* with three *f*s, which shows that the word is more clearly made up of the two words *Schiff* and *fahrt*.

    c. Some possible objections might include the following: It will be costly and difficult to replace all public signage. It might be very difficult or impossible to force people to use a new spelling system, which might lead to a situation where there are two parallel systems instead of the new system replacing the older system. Even the youngest generation, which could theoretically be taught only the new system in school, will need to know how to read the older system since there are so many materials already published using that system.

    d. Some might argue that the spelling reform could take hold within the span of two or three generations, once those most resistant to the new system and attached to the old system have died. Others might argue that it is too difficult to ask people to change their writing system and that people might have emotional and sentimental attachments to a writing system that make this kind of change unlikely to happen.

    e. Other spelling reforms include: (1) Indonesian in 1947 and 1972; (2) Danish in 1948; (3) Portuguese in the early 20th century.

19. *Spelling rhyme.* Answers will vary. Here are five we found in Shakespeare's sonnets: *field / held* in Sonnet 2, *alone / gone* in Sonnet 4, *glass / was* in Sonnet 5, *age / pilgrimage* in Sonnet 7, and *ear / bear* in Sonnet 8. Two additional examples come from *The Pirates of Penzance* by Gilbert and Sullivan: *lot* [lat] is rhymed with *pilot* [paɪlət] and *gyrate* [ʤaɪret] is rhymed with *pirate* [pʰaɪrət].